BREAKTHROUGH
POWER

BREAKTHROUGH
POWER

A Daily Guide to an Extraordinary Life

DAVID YOUNG

Wind Runner Press
Round Rock, Texas

Published by Wind Runner Press
P.O. Box 5730, Round Rock, TX 78683

Printed in the United States of America

Breakthrough power : a daily guide to an extraordinary life / [compiled by] David Young. –1st ed.
    p. cm.
LCCN 2009935242
ISBN-13: 978-1-936179-00-8
ISBN-10: 1-936179-00-8
1. Success–Quotations, maxims, etc. 2. Conduct of life–Quotations, maxims, etc. I. Young, David, 1957-
PN6084.S78B74 2010   646.7
                                   QBI09-600147

Quantity discounts are available. For information, please write to Wind Runner Press, P.O. Box 5730, Round Rock, TX 78683.

Dedication

To my mother, Mina, and the memory of my father, Dayton, who taught me the value of hard work. And to my wife, Christina, who showed me the power of love.

Introduction

Do you have a goal or dream that seems out of reach? Maybe it's a career goal, a dream of being financially secure or the desire to make a significant contribution to society. Did you try before but fall short? Perhaps you read a book that explained the keys to success, got excited about the possibilities, tried to make the suggested changes, but struggled and lost your enthusiasm a few months later. If so, you're not alone. The road to success is usually under construction. Bumpy roads, stop-and-go traffic and countless detours can wear you down and leave you confused about what to do next. You need more than a few tips on how to succeed; you also need motivation to push forward when success seems far away or impossible. *Breakthrough Power* provides both. It provides tools for building a successful and rewarding life and daily motivation to help you persevere until you achieve your dreams.

For each day of the year, *Breakthrough Power* provides four great quotes, usually from people known for their outstanding accomplishments. Their insights are based on years of experience. You can read all four quotes in one minute, so you can squeeze them in before you start your breakthrough day.

The first quote is humorous, which will put you in a good mood, ready to face life's challenges. The second one will help you focus on the important things in life, such as developing integrity, building a strong family, making a difference in the lives of others, enjoying simple pleasures and finding time for renewal, all critical to laying an unshakeable foundation. The third quote will help you overcome the weaknesses and seemingly impossible circumstances that have held you back. And the forth one will help you seize the summits. These will encourage you to dream big, set goals, develop effective plans of action, follow through with superior work and persevere, even after setbacks or failures. In short, *Breakthrough Power* will help you leave a legacy of greatness and enjoy the journey along the way.

Dusty roads lead to the most interesting places. Dust off your dreams and enjoy the journey.

Start with a smile

Never tell a woman that you didn't realize she was pregnant unless you're certain that she is.

— *Dave Barry*

Focus on what's important

Character may be manifested in the great moments, but it is made in the small ones.

— *Phillips Brooks*

Break the barriers

I would never have amounted to anything were it not for adversity. I was forced to come up the hard way.

— *J.C. Penney*

Seize the summits

You must have long-range goals to keep you from being frustrated by short-range failures.

— *Charles Noble*

❧ January 2

Start with a smile
I've decided to never sky dive. It would scare the heck out of my dog.

> — *Gretchen Alexander, when asked if there is anything she wouldn't try as a blind woman*

Focus on what's important
When you're not thinking about yourself, you're usually happy.

> — *Al Pacino*

Break the barriers
Nothing in the world can take the place of persistence. Talent will not; nothing is more common than unsuccessful individuals with talent. Genius will not; unrewarded genius is almost a proverb. Education will not; the world is full of educated derelicts. Persistence and determination alone are omnipotent.

> — *Calvin Coolidge*

Seize the summits
Success is 99 percent failure.

> — *Soichire Honda*

Start with a smile
When a man says, "Honey, there are only two minutes left in the football game," it is the same amount of time as when his wife says, "Honey, I'll be ready in two minutes."

— *Ann Landers*

Focus on what's important
If a man is called to be a streetsweeper, he should sweep streets even as Michelangelo painted, or Beethoven composed music or Shakespeare wrote poetry. He should sweep streets so well that all the hosts of heaven and earth will pause to say, here lived a great streetsweeper who did his job well.

— *Martin Luther King, Jr.*

Break the barriers
A man learns to skate by staggering about making a fool of himself; indeed, he progresses in all things by making a fool of himself.

— *George Bernard Shaw*

Seize the summits
Whatever you can do or dream you can, begin it. Boldness has genius, power and magic in it.

— *Johann von Goethe*

Start with a smile

The human brain starts working the moment you are born and never stops until you stand up to speak in public.

— Sir George Jessel

Focus on what's important

Everything has its wonders, even darkness and silence, and I learn whatever state I may be in, therein to be content.

— Helen Keller

Break the barriers

The more concerned we become over the things we can't control, the less we will do with the things we can control.

— John Wooden

Seize the summits

Character is the ability to carry out a good resolution long after the excitement of the moment has passed.

— Cavett Robert

Start with a smile
A word to new brides: if you want to be remembered forever, don't write a thank-you note for a wedding gift.
— *Edward Rankin, Jr.*

Focus on what's important
The friend who holds your hand and says the wrong thing is made of dearer stuff than the one who stays away.
— *Barbara Kingsolver*

Break the barriers
Be so good they can't ignore you.
— *Jerry Dunn*

Seize the summits
The key to successful time management is doing the most important task first, and giving it your full concentration, to the exclusion of everything else.
— *Alex MacKenzie*

Start with a smile

Eloquence: The ability to describe Pamela Anderson without using one's hands.

— Michael Harkness

Focus on what's important

I have learned that people will forget what you said, people will forget what you did, but people will never forget how you made them feel.

— Maya Angelou

Break the barriers

Nurture your mind with great thoughts. To believe in the heroic makes heroes.

— Benjamin Disraeli

Seize the summits

All great and honorable actions are accompanied with great difficulties.

— William Bradford

Start with a smile

There are only two things that are really impossible: putting toothpaste back in the tube and getting off a mailing list.

— *Anonymous*

Focus on what's important

Look for ways to make your boss look good.

— *H. Jackson Brown, Jr.*

Break the barriers

What we learn to do, we learn by doing.

— *Aristotle*

Seize the summits

Set higher standards for your own performance than anyone around you, and it won't matter whether you have a tough boss or an easy one. It won't matter whether the competition is pushing you hard, because you'll be competing with yourself.

— *Rick Pitino*

Start with a smile
Make money and the whole world will conspire to call you a gentleman.

— Mark Twain

Focus on what's important
It is necessary for me to be extremely frugal for some time, till I have paid what I owe.

— Benjamin Franklin

Break the barriers
To ease another's heartache is to forget one's own.

— Abraham Lincoln

Seize the summits
If a man does not keep pace with his companions, perhaps it is because he hears a different drummer. Let him step to the music he hears, however measured or far away.

— Henry David Thoreau

Start with a smile

Leisure time is when your wife can't find you.

— Anonymous

Focus on what's important

The highest calling of a human being is unselfish love – to love without being loved back, without any self-interest.

— Reinhold Niebuhr

Break the barriers

Learning the truth about the value of relaxation and reflection didn't happen overnight, but I did learn. I've made the effort to take the frenzy and sense of emergency out of my daily life. I've made the effort to put playfulness, serenity and, dare I say, even laziness into my life. I consider the latter the most luxurious and definitely the most difficult.

— Joan Lunden

Seize the summits

Losing is a learning experience. It teaches you humility. It teaches you to work harder. It's also a powerful motivator.

— Yogi Berra

Start with a smile
I bought a tube of Krazy Glue and the label fell off.

— *Jay Leno*

Focus on what's important
The more money you have, the more problems you have. I went from having no money to making comparatively a lot and all I've had are problems. Life was simpler when I had no money, when I just barely survived.

— *Madonna*

Break the barriers
He has power who can keep silent in an argument, even though he is right.

— *Leo Tolstoy*

Seize the summits
People who chase their dreams do what they love and they go for greatness. Those kinds of dreams, the dreams that fill their minds with purposeful energy, are the most potent source of motivation I know.

— *Dr. Bob Rotella*

Start with a smile

The supervisor is the leader of the herd. When he's happy, his employees are happy. When he's upset, his employees are upset. When he's on vacation . . .

— Gene Perret

Focus on what's important

The happiness of married life depends upon making small sacrifices with readiness and cheerfulness.

— John Selden

Break the barriers

You may succeed when others do not believe in you, but never when you do not believe in yourself.

— Anonymous

Seize the summits

I have never known a really successful man who deep in his heart did not understand the grind, the discipline it takes to win.

— Vince Lombardi

Start with a smile

My dental hygienist is cute. Every time I visit, I eat a whole package of Oreo cookies while waiting in the lobby. Sometimes she has to cancel the rest of her afternoon appointments.

— *Steven Wright*

Focus on what's important

Quiet play can bring the child in you to the surface. I once saw an executive in the business-class section of an airplane pull a large coloring book from his briefcase and set to work. "My hobby," he told me as I shot him a questioning glance. Try it. Buy a box of crayons – splurge on the super-duper box of sixty-four colors – and spend an hour coloring.

— *Thomas Kinkade*

Break the barriers

If you can't excel with talent, triumph with effort.

— *Dave Weinbaum*

Seize the summits

Nobody who ever gave his best regretted it.

— *George Halas*

Start with a smile
"Do you know someone perfect? Of course, not one of us does."
But then a hand went up.
"Do you mean to say you know of someone perfect?"
"Yes, my wife's first husband."

— *Anonymous*

Focus on what's important
If you can't think of something nice to say, keep thinking.

— *Criswell Freeman*

Break the barriers
A strong body makes the mind strong.

— *Thomas Jefferson*

Seize the summits
No matter how small and unimportant what we are doing may seem, if we do it well, it may soon become the step that will lead us to better things.

— *Channing Pollock*

Start with a smile
I want a man who is kind and understanding. Is that too much to ask of a millionaire?

— Zsa Zsa Gabor

Focus on what's important
Forgiveness does not change the past, but it does enlarge the future.

— Paul Boese

Break the barriers
The longer I live, the more beautiful life becomes.

— Frank Lloyd Wright

Seize the summits
A man watches his pear tree, day after day, impatient for the ripening of the fruit. Let him attempt to force the process, and he may spoil both fruit and tree. But let him patiently wait, and the ripe pear, at length, falls into his lap.

— Abraham Lincoln

Start with a smile

Thank heaven we don't get all the government we pay for.

— *Will Rogers*

Focus on what's important

Gratitude. More aware of what you have than what you don't. Recognizing the treasure in the simple – a child's hug, fertile soil, a golden sunset. Relishing in the comfort of the common – a warm bed, a hot meal, a clean shirt.

— *Max Lucado*

Break the barriers

If all misfortunes were laid in one common heap whence everyone must take an equal portion, most people would be contented to take their own and depart.

— *Socrates*

Seize the summits

Only those who risk going too far can possibly find out how far one can go.

— *T.S. Eliot*

Start with a smile
A shortcut is the longest distance between two points.

— Anonymous

Focus on what's important
To have a passion for life is not only to wake up in the morning and hear birds singing, but it is taking the time to open the window to see where they are perched on the tree. That is one of the side benefits of passion. You pay attention to details. And it is the details that determine the quality of life.

— Neil Simon

Break the barriers
All I have seen teaches me to trust the Creator for all I have not seen.

— Ralph Waldo Emerson

Seize the summits
As for worrying about what other people might think – forget it. They aren't concerned about you. They're too busy worrying about what you and other people think of them.

— Michael le Boeuf

Start with a smile

Middle age is when your broad mind and narrow waist begin to change places.

— E. Joseph Cossman

Focus on what's important

What will your children remember? Moments spent listening, talking, playing and sharing together may be the most important times of all.

— Gloria Gaither

Break the barriers

Before a person can achieve the kind of life he wants, he must think, act, walk, talk and conduct himself in all of his affairs as would the person he wishes to become.

— Zig Zigler

Seize the summits

You must do the things today that others will not do so that you can have the things tomorrow that others will not have.

— Anonymous

Start with a smile

Map: Handy schematic representation of all the various roads in the area which, unlike the one you are now on or are currently looking for, are large enough to be shown on a map.

— Henry Beard and Roy McKie

Focus on what's important

Humility is not thinking less of yourself; it is thinking of yourself less.

— Rick Warren

Break the barriers

The world hates change, yet it is the only thing that has brought progress.

— Charles Kettering

Seize the summits

When everybody tells you that you are being idealistic or impractical, consider the possibility that everybody could be wrong about what is right for you.

— Gilbert Kaplan

Start with a smile
Knowing all about baseball is just about as profitable as being a good whittler.

— *Kin Hubbard*

Focus on what's important
Making a decision usually means taking one of two roads. One is doing the right thing. To take the other road, you have to sit back and spin a story around the decision or action you are taking. If you find yourself thinking up an elaborate justification for what you are doing, you are not doing the right thing.

— *Wayne Sales*

Break the barriers
To acquire knowledge, one must study; but to acquire wisdom, one must observe.

— *Marilyn vos Savant*

Seize the summits
Careful planning helps us maintain a sense of perspective, purpose and ordered priorities.

— *Stephen Covey*

Start with a smile

The key to success? Work hard, stay focused and marry a Kennedy.

— Arnold Schwarzenegger

Focus on what's important

Do not run after happiness, but seek to do good, and you will find that happiness will run after you.

— James Clarke

Break the barriers

The secret of survival is not simply enjoying life's joys and enduring its sorrows, it is in sharing both with others. We gain perspective by having somebody at our side. We gain objectivity. We gain courage in threatening situations. Having others near tempers our dogmatism and softens our intolerance. We gain another opinion.

— Charles Swindoll

Seize the summits

Stay committed to your decisions, but stay flexible in your approach. It's the end you're after.

— Anthony Robbins

Start with a smile

I got into an argument with my girlfriend inside a tent. A tent is not a good place for an argument. I tried to walk out on her and had to slam the flap.

— *Mitch Hedberg*

Focus on what's important

Hang out with people in the slow lane. Take the time to learn, make friends, appreciate things. The fast life is over quick.

— *Rudy Sanchez*

Break the barriers

The greater the difficulty, the more glory in surmounting it.

— *Epicurus*

Seize the summits

The moment you commit and quit holding back, all sorts of unforeseen incidents, meetings and material assistance will rise up to help you. The simple act of commitment is a powerful magnet for help.

— *Napoleon Hill*

Start with a smile

You can quietly watch a game with your buddy for hours without ever thinking, "He's mad at me."

> — *Anonymous, on why it's great to be a man*

Focus on what's important

No matter how horrible someone is, there is always something about them that is good. Your job is to find that good bit and highlight it, speak about it, draw attention to it.

> — *Richard Templar*

Break the barriers

You can't create the perception you are content with your knowledge base. Things are moving too quickly. You must do everything in your power to keep up. If you don't, you are all but hanging a sign around your neck and labeling yourself as obsolete.

> — *Rick Pitino*

Seize the summits

A hard beginning hath a good ending.

> — *James Howell*

Start with a smile

Intuition: That strange instinct that tells a woman she is right, whether she is or not.

— *Anonymous*

Focus on what's important

Success is waking up in the morning and bounding out of bed because there's something out there that you love to do, that you believe in, that you're good at – something that's bigger than you are, and you can hardly wait to get at it again.

— *Whit Hobbs*

Break the barriers

Financial freedom comes to people who save 10 percent or more of their income throughout their lifetime.

— *Brian Tracy*

Seize the summits

Decide that you want it more than you are afraid of it.

— *Bill Cosby*

Start with a smile
Most people want to be delivered from temptation but would like it to keep in touch.

— Robert Orben

Focus on what's important
Bless those who persecute you; bless and do not curse.

— Romans 12:14

Break the barriers
If people knew how hard I worked to gain my mastery, it wouldn't seem so wonderful.

— Michelangelo

Seize the summits
After investigating a problem in all directions, ideas come unexpectedly, without effort, like an inspiration.

— H.L. von Helmholtz

Start with a smile

I never know what to get my father for his birthday. Once I gave him a hundred dollars and said, "Buy yourself something that will make your life easier." So he went out and bought a present for my mother.

— Rita Rudner

Focus on what's important

The less you talk, the more you're listened to.

— Abigail Van Buren

Break the barriers

The iron crown of suffering precedes the golden crown of glory.

— Anonymous

Seize the summits

If your actions create a legacy that inspires others to dream more, learn more, do more and become more, then you are an excellent leader.

— Dolly Parton

Start with a smile

If you want to hear the whole truth about yourself, anger your neighbor.

— *Anonymous*

Focus on what's important

The New Testament is the best book the world has ever known or will know.

— *Charles Dickens*

Break the barriers

Courage means putting at risk your immediate self-interest for what you believe is right.

— *Derrick Bell*

Seize the summits

If you don't fail now and again, it's a sign you're playing it safe.

— *Woody Allen*

Start with a smile
Like so many contemporary philosophers, he especially enjoyed giving helpful advice to people who were happier than he was.
— *Tom Lehrer*

Focus on what's important
I'd rather be a failure at something I love than a success at something I hate.

— *George Burns*

Break the barriers
To be prepared is half the victory.

— *Miguel de Cervantes*

Seize the summits
You have set yourself a difficult task, but you will succeed if you persevere.

— *Helen Keller*

Start with a smile

When two people go to bed together at the same time, the one that snores will fall asleep first.

— Laurence Peter

Focus on what's important

I know of no great men except those who have rendered great service to the human race.

— Voltaire

Break the barriers

Every successful man I have heard of has done the best he could with conditions as he found them, and not waited until the next year for better.

— Edgar Howe

Seize the summits

We can learn from past failures and mistakes, but we shouldn't get stuck there. We can keep future goals in mind, but we shouldn't get stuck there, either. The only way to reach our potential is to focus on what we must do now – this moment, this day – to perform effectively and win.

— Joe Torre

Start with a smile

Accordion: A bagpipe with pleats.

— Anonymous

Focus on what's important

Never judge or underestimate people by their physical appearance. Successful people come in all weights, heights, shapes, sizes and colors.

— Brian Koslow

Break the barriers

Character – the willingness to accept responsibility for one's own life – is the source from which self-respect springs.

— Joan Didion

Seize the summits

Every memorable act in the world is a triumph of enthusiasm. Nothing great was ever achieved without it because it gives any challenge or any occupation, no matter how frightening or difficult, a new meaning. Without enthusiasm you are doomed to a life of mediocrity but with it you can accomplish miracles.

— Og Mandion

Start with a smile
There is one thing more exasperating than a wife who can cook and won't, and that is the wife who can't cook and will.

— Robert Frost

Focus on what's important
No man ever yet became great by imitation.

— Samuel Johnson

Break the barriers
It is the studying that you do after your school days that really counts. Otherwise, you know only that which everyone else knows.

— Henry Doherty

Seize the summits
Satisfaction lies in the effort, not in the attainment. Full effort is full victory.

— Màhatma Gandhi

Start with a smile
The parable of the Good Samaritan for sociologists: A man was attacked and left bleeding in a ditch. Two sociologists passed by, and one said to the other, "We must find the man who did this – he needs help."

— *Anonymous*

Focus on what's important
Give not advice without being asked; and when desired, do it briefly.

— *George Washington*

Break the barriers
Self-esteem is like a difficult-to-cultivate flower. It requires frequent nurturing that occurs when you keep your word and follow through on your promises.

— *Derrick Bell*

Seize the summits
There's no such thing as not enough time if you're doing what you want to do.

— *Robert Half*

Start with a smile

Parking space: An unoccupied place on the other side of the street.

— Anonymous

Focus on what's important

The secret of happiness? Enjoy small pleasures.

— Samuel Smiles

Break the barriers

When you eat to excess, illnesses enter your body. Behave in such a way that when you finish your dinner, you want to eat a little more.

— Leo Tolstoy

Seize the summits

Beware of little expenses, a small leak will sink a great ship.

— Benjamin Franklin

Start with a smile

Why do you press harder on a remote control when you know the battery is dead?

— Anonymous

Focus on what's important

How do you say "I love you?" Often, and loud!

— Leo Buscaglia

Break the barriers

Use what talents you have; the woods would have little music if no birds sang their song except those who sang best.

— Oliver Wilson

Seize the summits

Sometimes when I consider what tremendous consequences come from little things, I am tempted to think there are no little things.

— Ralph Waldo Emerson

Start with a smile

Intellectual: A guy who can keep his mind on a book at a beach.

— *Anonymous*

Focus on what's important

If I can stop one heart from breaking,
　　I shall not live in vain:
　　If I can ease one life the aching,
　　Or cool one pain,
　　Or help one fainting robin
　　Unto his nest again,
　　I shall not live in vain.

— *Emily Dickinson*

Break the barriers

A man too busy to take care of his health is like a mechanic too busy to take care of his tools.

— *Cicero*

Seize the summits

If you want to be happy, set a goal that commands your thoughts, liberates your energy and inspires your hopes.

— *Andrew Carnegie*

Start with a smile

I couldn't eat toast for years when I was drinking heavily, because it was too noisy.

— *Clarissa Dickson-Wright*

Focus on what's important

Strong and bitter words indicate a weak cause.

— *Victor Hugo*

Break the barriers

To be upset over what you don't have is to waste what you do have.

— *Ken Keyes, Jr.*

Seize the summits

Success in anything in this world is 75 percent mental. In our league, most times the teams are evenly matched in ability and physically. And it is usually the team that is best mentally prepared on that particular day which wins the ballgame.

— *Vince Lombardi*

Start with a smile

Whatever else you do, sign it. If you do that, we will know which way to hold it.

> — *Auguste Rodin, to Picasso, regarding his latest painting*

Focus on what's important

You can tell more about a person by what he says about others than you can by what others say about him.

> — *Leo Aikman*

Break the barriers

He who conquers others is strong;
He who conquers himself is mighty.

> — *Lao Tzu*

Seize the summits

Opportunity follows struggle. It follows effort. It follows hard work. It doesn't come before.

> — *Shelby Steele*

Start with a smile
Sympathy: What you give a friend or relative when you don't want to lend him money.

— Anonymous

Focus on what's important
We read books to find out who we are. What other people, real or imaginary, do and think and feel is an essential guide to our understanding of what we ourselves are and may become.

— Ursula Le Guin

Break the barriers
Humor is the best therapy.

— Norman Cousins

Seize the summits
Without a plan we keep covering old territory.

— Rick Pitino

Start with a smile

"Dating" simply means "going out with a potential mate and doing a lot of fun things that the two of you will never do again if you actually get married."

— Dave Barry

Focus on what's important

You can make more friends in two months by becoming interested in other people than you can in two years of trying to get other people interested in you.

— Dale Carnegie

Break the barriers

When pain doesn't go away, endurance increases.

— T.D. Jakes

Seize the summits

On the whole, it is patience which makes the final difference between those who succeed or fail.

— John Ruskin

Start with a smile
Success: Something that always comes faster to the man your wife almost married.

— *Anonymous*

Focus on what's important
Obey your leaders and submit to their authority. They keep watch over you as men who must give an account. Obey them so that their work will be a joy, not a burden, for that would be of no advantage to you.

— *Hebrews 13:17*

Break the barriers
Every man, however intelligent, needs the advice of some wise friend in the affairs of life.

— *Plautus*

Seize the summits
Courage is doing what you're afraid to do. There can be no courage unless you're scared.

— *Eddie Rickenbacker*

Start with a smile

He is so shaggy. People are amazed when he gets up and they suddenly realize they have been talking to the wrong end.

— *Elizabeth Jones*

Focus on what's important

We should consider every day lost in which we have not danced at least once.

— *Friedrich Nietzsche*

Break the barriers

When you take a risk and accept the challenge of change, you stretch yourself. You build reserves of courage that will grow with you. The next challenge isn't as scary. The ground is more familiar, the obstacles don't loom as large and you're more agile in scaling them.

— *Vickie Milazzo*

Seize the summits

All that is necessary to break the spell of inertia and frustration is this: Act as if it were impossible to fail.

— *Dorthea Brande*

Start with a smile

Have you ever taken anything out of the clothes basket because it had become, relatively, the cleaner thing?

— *Katherine Whitehorn*

Focus on what's important

Persistent love – like the dripping of water on a rock – can wear away a person's resistance. It's nearly impossible to stay angry with or emotionally distant from someone who unconditionally loves and values you.

— *Gary and Norma Smalley*

Break the barriers

Cast all your cares on God; that anchor holds.

— *Lord Alfred Tennyson*

Seize the summits

Most of the world's useful work is done by people who are pressed for time, or are tired, or don't feel well.

— *Douglas Freeman*

Start with a smile

A man may be a fool and not know it – but not if he is married.

— *H.L. Mencken*

Focus on what's important

Heroes are people who rise to the occasion and slip quietly away.

— *Tom Brokaw*

Break the barriers

A capacity and taste for reading gives access to whatever has been discovered by others. It is the key, or one of the keys, to the already solved problems. And not only so; it gives a relish and facility for successfully pursuing the unsolved ones.

— *Abraham Lincoln*

Seize the summits

The most absurd and reckless aspirations have sometimes led to extraordinary success.

— *Marquis de Vauvenargues*

Start with a smile

I simply cannot find the words to tell you how superb you were.
Try.

— Claire Trevor and Judith Anderson

Focus on what's important

Generally speaking, we are all happier when we are still striving
for achievement than when the prize is in our hands.

— Margot Fonteyn

Break the barriers

Don't overreact to current troubles; remember past accomplishments that help keep your confidence high.

— Joe Torre

Seize the summits

Whatever your hand finds to do, do it with all your might.

— Ecclesiastes 9:10

Start with a smile
When you start having lunch and actually eating, it's already over.

— Erica Jong, on love

Focus on what's important
Never seem more learned than the people you are with. Wear your learning like a pocket watch and keep it hidden. Do not pull it out to count the hours, but give the time when you are asked.

— Lord Chesterfield

Break the barriers
Not being beautiful was the true blessing. It forced me to develop my inner resources. The pretty girl has a handicap to overcome.

— Golda Meir

Seize the summits
If one advances confidently in the direction of his dreams, and endeavors to live the life which he has imagined, he will meet with success unexpected in common hours.

— Henry David Thoreau

Start with a smile
Economists are people who see something work in practice and wonder if it would work in theory.

— Ronald Reagan

Focus on what's important
Our greatest wealth is not measured in terms of riches but relationships.

— Oliver Cromwell

Break the barriers
Always aim high. Don't settle for what you know you can accomplish. Challenge yourself to pursue the impossible, and you'll go farther than you can ever imagine.

— Margaret Spellings

Seize the summits
The secret of success is constancy of purpose.

— Benjamin Disraeli

Start with a smile

I rang the bell of this small bed-and-breakfast place, whereupon a lady appeared at a window. "What do you want?" she asked. "I want to stay here," I replied. "Well, stay there then," she said and closed the window.

— Chic Murray

Focus on what's important

We can measure our servant's heart by how we respond when others treat us like servants.

— Rick Warren

Break the barriers

Should-haves solve nothing. It's the next thing to happen that needs thinking about.

— Alexandra Ripley

Seize the summits

When a decision has to be made, make it. There is no totally right time for anything.

— General George Patton

Start with a smile
Man is born with a tendency to detect a maximum of contributory negligence in other people's misfortunes, and nothing but blind chance in his own.

— Arthur Schnitzler

Focus on what's important
The more right you are, the more careful you should be to express your opinion tactfully. The other fellow never likes to be proven wrong.

— John Luther

Break the barriers
When looking for a job, tell the man what you can do for him, not how good you are.

— Martin Vanbee

Seize the summits
Never look back unless you want to go that way.

— Anonymous

Start with a smile
To me old age is always fifteen years older than I am.

— *Bernard Baruch*

Focus on what's important
The best servant does his work unseen.

— *Oliver Wendell Holmes*

Break the barriers
Do not believe that he who seeks to comfort you lives untroubled among the simple and quiet words that sometimes do you good. His life has much difficulty and sadness and remains far behind yours. Were it otherwise he would never have been able to find those words.

— *Rainer Rilke*

Seize the summits
Many people go through life putting off their joy and happiness. To them, goal setting means that "someday," after they achieve something, only then will they be able to enjoy life to the fullest. The truth is that if we decide to be happy now, we'll automatically achieve more.

— *Anthony Robbins*

Start with a smile
She laughs at everything you say. Why? Because she has fine teeth.

— Benjamin Franklin

Focus on what's important
To have read the greatest works of any great poet, to have beheld or heard the greatest works of any great painter or musician, is a possession added to the best things of life.

— Algernon Swinburne

Break the barriers
I use running to gain energy. If you're going to succeed in a very, very difficult profession, you'd better be fit.

— Israel Horovitz

Seize the summits
You may be disappointed if you fail, but you are doomed if you don't try.

— Beverly Sills

Start with a smile

My husband forgot my birthday and my anniversary. I didn't feel bad. On the contrary. Give me a guilty husband any day. Some of my best outfits come from his guilt.

— Betty Walker

Focus on what's important

He that returns a good for evil obtains the victory.

— Thomas Fuller

Break the barriers

Learn as much by writing as by reading.

— Lord Acton

Seize the summits

Decisions are easier when you set goals for your life. This is because the decisions made are based on those goals. If you know where you're going and what you're seeking, then the decisions you make should be easier, because you'll make them with those goals in mind.

— Lewis Timberlake

Start with a smile
Famous last words: Believe me, nobody'll dress up.

— *Anonymous*

Focus on what's important
All you have to do is go to a hospital and hear all the simple blessings that people never before realized were blessings – being able to urinate, to sleep on your side, to be able to swallow, to scratch an itch, etc. Could exercises in deprivation educate us faster about all our blessings?

— *Abraham Maslow*

Break the barriers
Most people who never achieve their dreams are not held back by difficult circumstances. They are not stopped by lack of opportunity or because strong men oppose them. They fail simply because they don't believe they can succeed.

— *Pat Williams*

Seize the summits
Constant effort and frequent mistakes are the stepping-stones of genius.

— *Elbert Hubbard*

Start with a smile

When we ask advice we are usually looking for an accomplice.
— *Charles de La Grange*

Focus on what's important

Assume a cheerfulness you do not feel and shortly you will feel the cheerfulness you assumed.

— *Chinese proverb*

Break the barriers

If I had my life to live over, I would have gone to bed when I was sick instead of pretending the earth would go into a holding pattern if I weren't there for the day.

— *Erma Bombeck*

Seize the summits

It seemed like whenever there was a problem in our family, my mother would bring out the toothpicks. We'd each get one. Then, she'd tell us to try and break them. We did it easily, of course. Then she'd hand each of us nine toothpicks bunched together. "Now, break them."

None of us could do it.

"As long as you stay together, nobody can break you down, either," she'd say.

— *Isiah Thomas*

Start with a smile

You know you're too obsessed with money if during a private audience with the Pope, all you can think is "I wonder what this cat's pullin' down?"

— Dennis Miller

Focus on what's important

Don't compare yourself to somebody else, especially materially. If I'm worrying about the other guy and what he's doing, about what he's making, about all the attention he's getting, I'm not going to be able to do what I'm capable of doing. It's a guaranteed way to make yourself miserable.

— John Wooden

Break the barriers

Curiosity is the key to making dreams come true.

— Walt Disney

Seize the summits

Our main business is not to see what lies dimly at a distance, but to do what lies clearly at hand.

— Thomas Carlyle

Start with a smile
If a man yells in the woods and no woman hears him, is he still wrong?

— *Anonymous*

Focus on what's important
Whoever is careless with the truth in small matters cannot be trusted with important matters.

— *Albert Einstein*

Break the barriers
A person without a sense of humor is like a wagon without springs, jolted by every pebble in the road.

— *Henry Ward Beecher*

Seize the summits
You have to learn that your dedication to hard work will pay off. I can promise you that. Because the world loves people who work hard at everything they do. The world notices those people and rewards them for that dedication. It might not be an immediate financial reward, but you will get something.

— *Russell Simmons*

Start with a smile

Free verse: A device for making poetry easier to write and harder to read.

— *H.L. Mencken*

Focus on what's important

I don't know what the big deal is about old age. Old people who shine from inside look 10 to 20 years younger.

— *Dolly Parton*

Break the barriers

The achievement of goals does not provide an ongoing sense of happiness. On the contrary, if one depends upon ultimate triumph for his happiness, he is destined to experience a tremendous letdown after the short-term euphoria of victory wears off. Real happiness lies in the striving toward goals. You have to have a purpose in life that does not fade away once you achieve a goal or reach a milestone.

— *Robert Ringer*

Seize the summits

Many times during auditions, I was told that I couldn't carry a note with a bucket, and that I sure couldn't play the piano.

— *Ray Charles*

Start with a smile

I was going to buy a copy of *The Power of Positive Thinking,* and then I thought: *What good would that do?*

— *Ronnie Shakes*

Focus on what's important

Save a part of your income and begin now, for the man with a surplus controls circumstances, and the man without a surplus is controlled by circumstances.

— *Henry Buckley*

Break the barriers

If you have faith in your future, you will have power in your present.

— *John Maxwell*

Seize the summits

The only life worth living is the adventurous life. Of such a life, the dominant characteristic is that it is unafraid. It is unafraid of what other people think. It does not adapt either its pace or its objectives to the pace and objectives of its neighbors. It thinks its own thoughts, it reads its own books, it develops its own hobbies and it is governed by its own conscience.

— *Raymond Fosdick*

Start with a smile
Timing has a lot to do with the outcome of a rain dance.

— *Anonymous*

Focus on what's important
Enjoy the little things, for one day you may look back and realize they were the big things.

— *Robert Brault*

Break the barriers
Thoughts are the thermostat that regulates what we accomplish in life. My body responds and reacts to the input from my mind. If I feed my mind upon doubt, disbelief and discouragement, that is precisely the kind of day my body will experience. If I adjust my thermostat forward to thoughts filled with vision, vitality and victory, I can count on that kind of day.

— *Charles Swindoll*

Seize the summits
All of the mistakes I ever made in my life were when I wanted to say No, and said Yes.

— *Moss Hart*

Start with a smile

I get paid for seeing that my clients have every break the law allows. I have knowingly defended a number of guilty men. But the guilty never escape unscathed. My fees are sufficient punishment for anyone.

— *F. Lee Bailey*

Focus on what's important

To love is to find pleasure in the happiness of the person loved.
— *Gottfried Leibniz*

Break the barriers

Keep a record of the times you've triumphed over misfortune. It will assure you that you can do so again. Remember your moments of joy and happiness. They will serve as a reservoir of strength when you most need it.

— *Leo Buscaglia*

Seize the summits

When you have a number of disagreeable duties to perform, always do the most disagreeable first.

— *Anonymous*

Start with a smile

Have you noticed? Anyone driving faster than you is an idiot, and anyone driving slower than you is a moron.

— *George Carlin*

Focus on what's important

Do not judge, and you will not be judged. Do not condemn, and you will not be condemned. Forgive, and you will be forgiven.

— *Luke 6:37*

Break the barriers

Every man like myself, who never went to college, can largely make up for that lack by reading the wise sayings of the great men of the past, who gladly left their wisdom and experience in proverbs for us who follow them.

— *Sir Winston Churchill*

Seize the summits

It's a simple fact: The opportunities of the moment often can't be deferred. We either say yes – now – or we are saying no. If we want to unwrap the gifts that life gives us, we need to be willing, at least occasionally, to accept the package and tear at the wrapping with gusto and abandon.

— *Thomas Kinkade*

Start with a smile

I have six locks on my door, all in a row, and when I go out I only lock every other lock. Because I figure no matter how long somebody stands there and picks the locks, they're always locking three.

— *Elayne Boosler*

Focus on what's important

I don't know the key to success, but the key to failure is trying to please everyone.

— *Bill Cosby*

Break the barriers

He who cannot accept reproof cannot become great.

— *Rabbi Nachman of Braslav*

Seize the summits

When I am living and working in harmony with my mission, my mind chatter and second-guessing stops. Life seems to flow smoothly. Even when challenges appear, they seem to be lessons on my journey instead of barriers or warnings to turn back. I am enthusiastic about what I am doing and feel energetic and at peace.

— *Marilyn Tam*

Start with a smile
It's a recession when your neighbor loses his job; it's a depression when you lose yours.

— *Harry S. Truman*

Focus on what's important
Fame is a pearl many dive for and only few bring up. Even when they do, it is not perfect and they sigh for more, and lose better things in struggling for them.

— *Louisa May Alcott*

Break the barriers
Opportunity is missed by most people because it is dressed in overalls, and looks like work.

— *Thomas Edison*

Seize the summits
The way to get ahead in this world is to do whatever work you are doing well, then you will be picked to do some other job that is not being done well.

— *Samuel Vauclair*

March 2

Start with a smile
Beware of the conversationalist who adds "in other words." He is merely starting afresh.

— *Christopher Morley*

Focus on what's important
I was the general in the war to save Chrysler. I began by reducing my salary to $1.00 a year. Leadership means setting an example.

— *Lee Iacocca*

Break the barriers
He cannot speak well that cannot hold his tongue.

— *Thomas Fuller*

Seize the summits
In my youth I stressed freedom, and in my old age I stressed order. I have made the great discovery that liberty is a product of order.

— *Will Durant*

Start with a smile
Some waiters discuss the menu with you as if they were sharing wisdom picked up in the Himalayas.

— Seymour Britchky

Focus on what's important
When a happy person comes into the room, it is as if another candle has been lit.

— Ralph Waldo Emerson

Break the barriers
Experience is not what happens to a man. It is what a man does with what happens to him.

— Aldous Huxley

Seize the summits
I always laugh when people praised me as an overnight success. Overnight plus nine years of training, sacrifice, hard work and discipline was more like it.

— Mary Lou Retton

Start with a smile
And now for my next trick. I'm going to make my boyfriend disappear. I say the magic word: opera.

— Lea Thompson

Focus on what's important
Consider how hard it is to change yourself and you'll understand what little chance you have of changing others.

— Jacob Braude

Break the barriers
The more excited you are about accomplishing something that is important to you, the more excited others will be about helping you do it. Emotions are contagious. The more passion you have for your life and your activities, the more charisma you will have, and the more cooperation you will gain from others.

— Andrew Wood and Brian Tracy

Seize the summits
Of all the liars in the world, sometimes the worst are your own fears.

— Rudyard Kipling

Start with a smile
It's supposed to do that.

— Computer help-line response

Focus on what's important
Happy people seldom think of happiness. They are too busy losing their lives in the meaningful sacrifices of service.

— David Augsburger

Break the barriers
Influence doesn't come to us instantaneously. It grows by stages.

— John Maxwell

Seize the summits
Honest work bears a lovely face, for it is the father of pleasure and the mother of good fortune. It is the keystone of prosperity and the sire of fame. And best of all, work is relief from sorrow and the handmaiden of happiness.

— Eugen Bertin

Start with a smile

Oh to be seventy again.

> — *Oliver Wendell Holmes, Jr., on seeing an attractive woman on his 90th birthday*

Focus on what's important

Give more and better service than you are paid for, and sooner or later you will receive compound interest from your investment. It is inevitable that every seed or useful service you sow will sprout and reward you with an abundant harvest.

> — *Napoleon Hill*

Break the barriers

Those who think they know everything, and so try to explain everything, often remain ignorant of many things that others could and would instruct them in, if they appeared less conceited.

> — *Benjamin Franklin*

Seize the summits

Assign a timeline to your goal. Unlike dreams, which are vague in both definition and time, goals require a particular schedule or calendar for their achievement.

> — *Phillip McGraw*

Start with a smile

Men don't care what's on TV. They only care what else is on TV.

— *Jerry Seinfeld*

Focus on what's important

Starting out to make money is the greatest mistake in life. Do what you feel you have a flair for doing, and if you are good enough at it, the money will come.

— *Greer Garson*

Break the barriers

God does not send us despair in order to kill us; he sends it in order to awaken us to new life.

— *Hermann Hesse*

Seize the summits

If you feel inordinately weighted down by things, it may be that you've forgotten why you're doing what you're doing. Sometimes tapping back into your reasons for carrying on will give you the strength to do so.

— *Richard Leider and David Shapiro*

Start with a smile
Going out with a jerky guy is kind of like having a piece of food caught in your teeth. All your friends notice it before you do.
— *Livia Squires*

Focus on what's important
Pay bad people with your goodness; fight their hatred with your kindness. Even if you do not achieve victory over other people, you will conquer yourself.
— *Henry Frederick Amiel*

Break the barriers
Use a budget not to inhibit and restrain yourself but to liberate and unleash your passion for something greater than the purchase that is tempting you in that moment.
— *T.D. Jakes*

Seize the summits
Wisely and slow. They stumble that run fast.
— *William Shakespeare*

Start with a smile

The quickest way to get rid of people is to lend them money.

— *Anita Blackman*

Focus on what's important

A book is a garden, an orchard, a storehouse, a party, a company by the way, a counselor, a multitude of counselors.

— *Henry Ward Beecher*

Break the barriers

Asking dumb questions is easier than correcting dumb mistakes.

— *Anonymous*

Seize the summits

Every minute spent in planning will save you two in execution.

— *Henry Kaiser*

Start with a smile

You never know how many friends you have until you rent a cottage at the beach.

— *Kraig Kristofferson*

Focus on what's important

Really good people are few and far between – don't let them go because of dumb mistakes or misunderstandings. The best friendships allow for a little flakiness.

— *Mindy Morgenstern*

Break the barriers

No one knows what he can do until he tries.

— *Publilius Syrus*

Seize the summits

Luck means the hardships which you have not hesitated to endure; the long nights you have devoted to work. Luck means the appointments you have never failed to keep, the airplanes you never failed to catch.

— *Margaret Clement*

Start with a smile

When a man brings his wife a gift for no reason, there's a reason.

— *Molly McGee*

Focus on what's important

The men who succeed best in public life are those who take the risk of standing by their own convictions.

— *James Garfield*

Break the barriers

There is no such thing as a self-made man. You will reach your goals only with the help of others.

— *George Shinn*

Seize the summits

Positive reinforcement is hugging your husband when he does a load of laundry. Negative reinforcement is telling him he used too much detergent.

— *Dr. Joyce Brothers*

Start with a smile

Budget: A mathematical confirmation of your suspicions.

— A.A. Latimer

Focus on what's important

Give thanks for everything you have. If you are bemoaning your lot, be grateful for all the things you don't have that you don't want.

— Marilyn Tam

Break the barriers

Worry never robs tomorrow of its sorrow, it only saps today of its joy.

— Leo Buscaglia

Seize the summits

It's important that you don't fear pressure: You should embrace it. It brings out the best in all of us. You want it every day of your working life. You want to feel that each day you are under a microscope, that you are involved in something that's important.

— Rick Pitino

Start with a smile

Remorse: A miscalculation of the chances of detection.

— Anonymous

Focus on what's important

The meaning of Sabbath is to celebrate time rather than space. Six days a week we live under the tyranny of things of space; on the Sabbath we try to become attuned to holiness in time. It is a day on which we are called upon to share in what is eternal, to turn from the results of creation to the mystery of creation.

— Abraham Heschel

Break the barriers

A wise man gets more use from his enemies than a fool from his friends.

— Baltasar Gracián

Seize the summits

The fear of failure is infinitely greater than failure. Failure gets me up earlier the next morning than success. If you get right back to work, yesterday's pain becomes today's inspiration.

— Neil Simon

Start with a smile

Why does my wife want me to go shopping with her? She knows I'm no good at it. She's going to want to do stuff like try different things on. Soon as she comes out of the dressing room with the first thing on, to me it's like a bank robbery. "Let's go!"

— *Ritch Shydner*

Focus on what's important

If you are patient in one moment of anger, you will escape a hundred days of sorrow.

— *Chinese proverb*

Break the barriers

Man's extremity is God's opportunity.

— *Thomas Adams*

Seize the summits

Often, what seems impossible in the short term becomes very possible in the long term if you persist. In order to succeed, we need to discipline ourselves to consistently think long term.

— *Anthony Robbins*

Start with a smile

The trouble with true humility is, you can't talk about it.

— *Michael Thomsett*

Focus on what's important

He who is not contented with little will never be satisfied with much.

— *Thomas Brooks*

Break the barriers

When asked your opinion of someone, something, somewhere, you need to find something good to say, something flattering and positive. There is ample evidence that being positive has many benefits but the most noticeable is that people will gravitate toward you and not even know why. That positive air about you is attractive. People like being around those who are upbeat, positive, happy and confident.

— *Richard Templar*

Seize the summits

A goal gives you confidence – it turns the meek to bold.

— *Don Decker*

Start with a smile
The meek shall inherit the earth – if that's all right with you.

— *Anonymous*

Focus on what's important
Leadership lies in sacrifice, self-denial, love, fearlessness and humility. And this is the distinction between great and little men.

— *Vince Lombardi*

Break the barriers
I am a little deaf, a little blind, a little impotent, and on top of this are two or three abominable infirmities, but nothing destroys my hope.

— *Voltaire*

Seize the summits
Work drives away the care and small troubles of life. The busy person has little time to brood or fret. Work brings the prizes in life. The reward of a thing well done isn't a plaque or a watch, or even a paycheck: It's the fact that you did it.

— *Ronda Beaman*

Start with a smile

I had one guy at a gas station in New York say to me, "Hey, you look like that Hugh Grant. No offense."

— *Hugh Grant*

Focus on what's important

The charity that hastens to proclaim its good deeds, ceases to be charity, and is only pride and ostentation.

— *William Hutton*

Break the barriers

Self-confidence is the hallmark of a champion – any champion.

— *Grantland Rice*

Seize the summits

All growth is a leap in the dark, an act without the benefit of experience.

— *Henry Miller*

Start with a smile
Stubbornness we deprecate,
    Firmness we condone.
    The former is my neighbor's trait,
    The latter is my own.

— Anonymous

Focus on what's important
You cannot truly listen to anyone and do anything else at the same time.

— M. Scott Peck

Break the barriers
When we're surrounded by things that look impossible, making a simple choice to do something that's possible is a powerful thing to do.

— Melody Beattie

Seize the summits
Wealth is largely a result of habit.

— John Astor

Start with a smile

He went for his annual physical. After the examination, the doctor said to his wife, "I don't like the looks of him."

The wife said, "I don't either, but he's so good to the kids."

— *Anonymous*

Focus on what's important

Deal with the faults of others as gently as with your own.

— *Henrichs*

Break the barriers

We only fear when we forget who walks beside us.

— *Hans Wilhelf*

Seize the summits

You were born with an inner guidance system that tells you when you are on or off purpose by the amount of joy you are experiencing. The things that bring you the greatest joy are in alignment with your purpose.

— *Jack Canfield*

Start with a smile
You go to the ballet and you see girls dancing on their tiptoes. Why don't they just get taller girls?

— *Greg Ray*

Focus on what's important
Children just don't fit into a "to do" list very well. It takes time to introduce them to good books – it takes time to fly kites and play ball and put together jigsaw puzzles. It takes time to listen.

— *James Dobson*

Break the barriers
Understand that often when you have searched in vain for a solution to a problem, you can find it by helping someone else solve his or her problem. By the time you have solved the other person's problem, you will have the insight to solve your own.

— *Napoleon Hill*

Seize the summits
The only way you can take control of your spending and determine your lifestyle priorities is with a budget.

— *T.D. Jakes*

Start with a smile

I'm now old enough to personally identify every object in antique stores.

— Anita Milner

Focus on what's important

Gossip needn't be false to be evil – there's a lot of truth that shouldn't be passed around.

— Frank Clark

Break the barriers

Some people are always grumbling because roses have thorns; I am thankful that thorns have roses.

— Alphonse Karr

Seize the summits

Think of winning as a puzzle. To achieve a "big" goal, assemble a large number of little accomplishments and make them fit perfectly together.

— Joe Torre

Start with a smile

If your husband has difficulty in getting to sleep, the words, "We need to talk about our relationship" may help.

— *Rita Rudner*

Focus on what's important

People who love each other are the happiest people in the world. We see that with our very poor people. They love their children and they love their families. They may have very little, in fact, they may not have anything, but they are happy people.

— *Mother Teresa*

Break the barriers

The moment you blame anyone for anything, your relationship and your personal power deteriorate.

— *Brian Koslow*

Seize the summits

Never let the urgent crowd out the important.

— *Kelly Walker*

Start with a smile
Old college classmate: Someone who's gotten so bald and fat
that he sees you at a class reunion and doesn't recognize you.
— *Anonymous*

Focus on what's important
I don't want people who want to dance, I want people who have
to dance.
— *George Balanchine*

Break the barriers
One person with a belief is equal to a force of ninety-nine who
have only interests.
— *John Stewart Mill*

Seize the summits
The key to activating the laws of success is for you to become
perfectly clear about what it is you want and exactly what it will
look like when you have achieved it. Just as you wouldn't attempt
to build a house without a plan, you wouldn't think of building
a great life without a clear list of the goals you wish to attain
and a written plan of action for the attainment of those goals.
— *Brian Tracy*

Start with a smile

Many an accident occurs when a man is driving under the influence of his wife.

— *Anonymous*

Focus on what's important

The best time for you to hold your tongue is the time you feel you must say something or bust.

— *Josh Billings*

Break the barriers

True leadership strengthens the followers. It is a process of teaching, setting an example and empowering others. If you seek to lead, your ability will ultimately be measured in the successes of those around you.

— *Dr. David Niven*

Seize the summits

All glory comes from daring to begin.

— *Eugene Ware*

Start with a smile
Middle age is when you hope nobody will invite you out next Saturday night.

— Anonymous

Focus on what's important
When you have read the Bible, you will know it is the word of God, because you will have found it the key to your own heart, your own happiness and your duty.

— Woodrow Wilson

Break the barriers
When we worry about going broke, getting sick or losing face, our focus is on ourselves. One way to reduce worrying is to shift gears, and focus on how you can help someone else.

— Dr. Suzanne Zoglio

Seize the summits
If you're not making mistakes, then you're not doing anything. I'm positive that a doer makes mistakes.

— John Wooden

Start with a smile
Question: What normally follows two days of rain?
Answer: Monday.

— *Ron Dentinger*

Focus on what's important
Before we set our hearts too much upon anything, let us examine how happy they are who already possess it.

— *François de La Rochefoucauld*

Break the barriers
Humor acts as a buffer against stress, an antidote to paralyzing perfectionism and a way to widen your perspective. It wards off depression and contributes to good health.

— *Roger Crawford*

Seize the summits
I don't wait for moods. You accomplish nothing if you do that. Your mind must know it has got to get down to work.

— *Pearl Buck*

Start with a smile

Gimme a table near a waiter.

— Henny Youngman

Focus on what's important

Never admit at work that you're tired, angry or bored.

— H. Jackson Brown, Jr.

Break the barriers

Most of my major disappointments have turned out to be blessings in disguise. So whenever anything bad does happen to me, I kind of sit back and feel, well, if I give this enough time, it'll turn out that this was good, so I won't worry about it too much.

— William Gaines

Seize the summits

To have a great purpose to work for, a purpose larger than ourselves, is one of the secrets of making life significant, for then the meaning and worth of the individual overflow his personal borders and survive his death.

— Will Durant

Start with a smile
Thank goodness for the scientist who said dead leaves help a lawn in the fall.

— *Anonymous*

Focus on what's important
Never is there a single instance when a lie can be justified.

— *Leo Tolstoy*

Break the barriers
A lean compromise is better than a fat lawsuit.

— *English proverb*

Seize the summits
If you have time and place for everything and do everything in its time and place, you will not only accomplish more but have more leisure than those who are always hurrying as if vainly attempting to overtake what has been lost.

— *Tryon Edwards*

Start with a smile

A positive attitude may not solve all your problems, but it will annoy enough people to make it worth the effort.

— *Herm Albright*

Focus on what's important

A good marriage is made up of two good forgivers.

— *Gigi Tchividjian*

Break the barriers

He that to what he sees, adds observation, and to what he reads, reflection, is on the right road to knowledge.

— *Charles Caleb Colton*

Seize the summits

No one ever did anything worth doing unless he was prepared to go on with it long after it became something of a bore.

— *Douglas Steere*

Start with a smile
Experience may be the best teacher but the one I had in grammar school was much prettier.

— Don McNeill

Focus on what's important
If you want to feel rich, just count all the things you have that money can't buy.

— Daniel Webster

Break the barriers
One of the marks of true greatness is the ability to develop greatness in others.

— J.C. McCauley

Seize the summits
You have to make sure that you don't treat your dreams like they are only dreams. You have to feel that they can become realities, too, or you will never think it's possible to attain them.

— Derek Jeter

Start with a smile

A toy company is releasing Teacher Barbie this week. Apparently, it's like Malibu Barbie – only she can't afford the Corvette.

— *Stephanie Miller*

Focus on what's important

You have not lived today until you have done something for someone who can never repay you.

— *John Bunyan*

Break the barriers

We are never defeated unless we give up on God.

— *Ronald Reagan*

Seize the summits

While striving to accomplish your goals, don't forget to enjoy the ride. Value what you are doing in the here and now, while continuing to work for something better.

— *Laurence Boldt*

Start with a smile

I went to watch Pavarotti once. He doesn't like it when you join in.

— *Mitch Miller*

Focus on what's important

Do not repay anyone evil for evil.

— *Romans 12:17*

Break the barriers

Lack of confidence is not the result of difficulty; the difficulty comes from a lack of confidence.

— *Seneca*

Seize the summits

I stood in front of a speech class and said, "I plan to make my living with my oratory skills, and I'd like to be a talk show host." There was a pause, then the most incredible laughter you've ever heard in your life.

— *Arsenio Hall*

❧ April 2

Start with a smile
She plunged into a sea of platitudes, and with the powerful breast stroke of a channel swimmer made her confident way towards the white cliffs of the obvious.

— *W. Somerset Maugham*

Focus on what's important
I still get wildly enthusiastic about little things. I play with leaves. I skip down the street and run against the wind.

— *Leo Buscaglia*

Break the barriers
Breakfast like a king, lunch like a prince, but dine like a pauper.

— *Gary Player*

Seize the summits
The first thing to go isn't the arm or legs. It's enthusiasm; it's passion. When that is gone, the player is through.

— *Pete Rose*

Start with a smile
When a man opens the car door for his wife, it's either a new car or a new wife.

— Prince Phillip

Focus on what's important
Nobody is bored when he is trying to make something that is beautiful, or to discover something that is true.

— William Inge

Break the barriers
Avoiding danger is no safer in the long run than outright exposure. Life is either a daring adventure or nothing.

— Helen Keller

Seize the summits
By making a daily plan you are instantly imposing some discipline on your time, and your actions. You lead the day rather than letting it be swept away from you. Day by day you are taking more control of your life.

— Rick Pitino

Start with a smile
In 1956 the population of Los Angeles was 2,243,901. It had risen to 2,811,801 by 1970. 1,650,917 of them are currently up for a series.
— *Fran Lebowitz*

Focus on what's important
Sweet success is a life brought alive by our full attention to the joys of the many small moments. It is an enduring sense of sufficiency that allows the most simple of things to soothe and reenergize us.
— *Dr. Paul Pearsall*

Break the barriers
The secret to staying young is to be interested, truly interested, in everything happening around you.
— *Charles VanBuskirk*

Seize the summits
I have no regrets because I know I did my best – all I could do.
— *Midori Ito*

Start with a smile
This stuff tastes awful. I could have made a fortune selling it in my health food store.

— *Woody Allen*

Focus on what's important
I didn't belong as a kid, and that always bothered me. If only I'd known that one day my differences would be an asset, then my early life would have been much easier.

— *Bette Midler*

Break the barriers
Faith is not a possession; it's a decision.

— *Alcoholics Anonymous saying*

Seize the summits
The minute you start talking about what you're going to do if you lose, you have lost.

— *George Shultz*

Start with a smile

I think Pringles' initial intention was to make tennis balls. But on the day the rubber was supposed to show up, a big truckload of potatoes arrived instead.

— Mitch Hedberg

Focus on what's important

To maintain integrity, do not make tough decisions alone. Ask questions, receive counsel, reflect and take a long-term view.

— Adrian Gostick and Dana Telford

Break the barriers

Every artist was first an amateur.

— Ralph Waldo Emerson

Seize the summits

Failure jolts us out of our routines and forces us to look for fresh approaches.

— Roger von Oech

Start with a smile

In America the young are always ready to give to those who are older than themselves the full benefits of their inexperience.

— *Oscar Wilde*

Focus on what's important

Happiness is inward, and not outward; and so, it does not depend on what we have, but on what we are.

— *Henry Van Dyke*

Break the barriers

Illness knocks a lot of nonsense out of us; it induces humility, cuts us down to size. Only when the gate grows narrow do some people discover their soul, their God, their life work.

— *Louis Bisch*

Seize the summits

Writing down your plans, goals and ideas makes them more real for you. Every step you take to define what you want and what you need to do to get it increases the chances that you will actually pursue these goals and someday achieve them.

— *Dr. David Niven*

Start with a smile

There are several ways in which to budget the family income, all of them unsatisfactory.

— *Robert Benchley*

Focus on what's important

Thousands upon thousands are yearly brought into a state of real poverty by their great anxiety not to be thought poor.

— *Robert Mallet*

Break the barriers

Welcome change as a friend; try to visualize new possibilities and the blessings they are bound to bring to you. If you stay interested in everything around you – in new ways of life, new people, new places and ideas – you'll stay young, no matter what your age. Never stop learning and never stop growing. This is the key to a rich and fascinating life.

— *Alexander De Seversky*

Seize the summits

The first step toward saving time is to find out how you've been spending it.

— *William Ruchti*

Start with a smile
"Would you call for help if I tried to kiss you?"
     "Do you need help?"

— Anonymous

Focus on what's important
To make the relationship go with a zing, you have to go back to square one and start being courteous again. Be thoughtful. Be complimentary. Give gifts without there being any reason for it. Ask questions to show you are interested in what your partner is saying.

— Richard Templar

Break the barriers
In seeking wisdom, the first step is silence, the second listening, the third remembering, the fourth practicing, the fifth – teaching others.

— Ibn Gabirol

Seize the summits
Success comes to those who know it isn't coming to them and who go out to get it.

— Frank Tyger

Start with a smile
How did I learn to dance? Simple – when I grew up there were six kids and only one bathroom.

— *Anonymous*

Focus on what's important
Nothing I've ever done has given me more joys and rewards than being a father to my children.

— *Bill Cosby*

Break the barriers
I am a woman who came from the cotton fields of the South. From there I was promoted to the washtub. From there I was promoted to the cook kitchen. And from there I promoted myself into the business of manufacturing hair products.

— *C.J. Walker*

Seize the summits
People forget how fast you did a job – but they remember how well you did it.

— *Howard Newton*

Start with a smile
Some people pay a compliment as if they expect a receipt.
— *Kin Hubbard*

Focus on what's important
It takes two people to have a marriage, but only one is necessary to change it. We end up feeling helpless in our marriages because we can't control our partners. The truth is that we need only learn to control ourselves.
— *Melvyn Kinder and Connell Cowan*

Break the barriers
You will keep moving toward your definite major purpose when you are surrounded by others who lend you aid and encouragement, whereas if you work alone, you will be inclined to slow down, become discouraged and quit.
— *Napoleon Hill*

Seize the summits
Only those who have the patience to do simple things perfectly will acquire the skill to do difficult things easily.
— *Johann von Schiller*

Start with a smile

Abstract art is a product of the untalented sold by the unprincipled to the utterly bewildered.

— *Al Capp*

Focus on what's important

I have long been in the habit of building joy-breaks into the course of my days – allowing myself certain small pleasures for the express purpose of keeping my attitude bright.

— *Thomas Kinkade*

Break the barriers

Instead of thinking about the fear and the negative consequences, concentrate on what you will get if you push yourself through this fear.

— *Anthony Robbins*

Seize the summits

He who hesitates is poor.

— *Mel Brooks*

Start with a smile
Don't lend money to friends – it causes amnesia.

— Anonymous

Focus on what's important
The beginning of love is to let those we love be perfectly themselves, and not to twist them to fit our own image. Otherwise we love only the reflection of ourselves we find in them.

— Thomas Merton

Break the barriers
An early morning walk is a blessing for the whole day.

— Henry David Thoreau

Seize the summits
Mental toughness is singleness of purpose and, once you have agreed upon the price that you and your family must pay for success, it enables you to forget that price. It enables you to ignore the minor hurts, the opponent's pressure and the temporary failures.

— Vince Lombardi

Start with a smile
When I want your opinion I'll give it to you.

— *Laurence Peter*

Focus on what's important
You will never have more happiness than you have discipline. The two are directly linked to each other. If you want to increase the level of fulfillment and happiness in a certain area of your life, increase your level of discipline in that area of your life.

— *Matthew Kelly*

Break the barriers
You need to have the expertise and the guidance of someone else. You cannot train yourself. The church is the gym of the soul.

— *Sylvester Stallone*

Seize the summits
Pain is only temporary. . . the benefits last forever.

— *Jack Canfield*

Start with a smile

April 15th is the day when you get to pay for the government you've been complaining about all year long.

— *Gene Perret*

Focus on what's important

No person was ever honored for what he received. Honor has been the reward for what he gave.

— *Calvin Coolidge*

Break the barriers

Success is the product of character. The development of your character is in your own hands, and poverty plus honest ambition is the best environment for character building.

— *Charlie Jones*

Seize the summits

Make no little plans. They have no magic to stir men's blood. Make big plans: aim high in hope and work.

— *Daniel Burnham*

Start with a smile

Junk is something you throw away three weeks before you need it.

— *Anonymous*

Focus on what's important

Blessings are like hugs from God to let you know how much He loves you. Counting blessings is like hugging God back.

— *Debby Boone*

Break the barriers

One reason we get so stressed when something goes wrong is that we focus only on what has gone wrong. We wish it hadn't happened and mumble about our rotten luck. Instead, try reframing a problem situation to see if there is any possible good in it.

— *Dr. Suzanne Zoglio*

Seize the summits

He who can take no interest in what is small, will take false interest in what is great.

— *John Ruskin*

Start with a smile

I don't consider myself bald. I'm simply taller than my hair.

— *Tom Sharp*

Focus on what's important

At the point in life where your talent meets the needs of the world, that is where God wants you to be.

— *Albert Schweitzer*

Break the barriers

Often the difference between a successful person and a failure is not one's better abilities or ideas, but the courage that one has to bet on one's ideas, to take a calculated risk – and to act.

— *Maxwell Maltz*

Seize the summits

It's the people who stop to consider their hurt and heartache who usually fall short of their goals. Some even drop out altogether just because they experience a little disappointment or sorrow. You've got to play through your pain if you want to make it where you're going.

— *George Foreman*

Start with a smile

Anyone who lives within his means suffers from a lack of imagination.

— Lionel Stander

Focus on what's important

We should seize every opportunity to give encouragement. Encouragement is oxygen to the soul.

— George Adams

Break the barriers

I always believe I can beat the best, achieve the best. I always see myself in the top position.

— Serena Williams

Seize the summits

Most of the significant contributions that have been made to society have been made by people who were tired.

— Sir Winston Churchill

Start with a smile

In ancient times, cats were worshipped as gods. They have never forgotten this.

— Terry Pratchett

Focus on what's important

One evening a little girl was taking a walk with her father. Looking up at the stars she exclaimed, "Daddy, if the wrong side of heaven is so beautiful, what must the right side be like?"

— Billy Graham

Break the barriers

Confidence is not thinking, "I just know that somehow things will turn out all right." It's thinking, "I know that if I do all the things necessary to succeed, I will succeed."

— Dr. Bob Rotella

Seize the summits

When you set priorities you are literally writing history in advance.

— Tom Skinner

❧ April 20

Start with a smile
To do is to be.

— *Descartes*

To be is to do.

— *Voltaire*

Do be do be do.

— *Frank Sinatra*

Focus on what's important
A great man is always willing to be little.

— *Ralph Waldo Emerson*

Break the barriers
All the genius I have is the fruit of labor.

— *Alexander Hamilton*

Seize the summits
To find a big opportunity, seek out a big problem.

— *H. Jackson Brown, Jr.*

Start with a smile

Thou shalt not committee.

> — *Tal Bonham, eleventh commandment*

Focus on what's important

Learning to say no to what you don't need really begins with learning to say yes to what you have. True simplicity, in other words, begins when you learn to enjoy the amazing abundance of what is already yours.

> — *Thomas Kinkade*

Break the barriers

Everybody talks about wanting to change things, but ultimately all you can do is fix yourself. And that's a lot. Because if you can fix yourself, it has a ripple effect.

> — *Rob Reiner*

Seize the summits

Nobody is going to wind you up every morning and give you a pep talk. So be a self-starter.

> — *Lou Holtz*

Start with a smile

An optimist is a man who will wink at a pretty girl and think that his wife won't see him.

— Anonymous

Focus on what's important

I argue very well. Ask any of my remaining friends. I can win an argument on any topic, against any opponent. People know this and steer clear of me at parties. Often, as a sign of their great respect, they don't even invite me.

— Dave Barry

Break the barriers

Adopt the policy that if you don't have the cash in hand, you can't afford it. With the exception of your home and possibly your car, don't buy on credit.

— Elaine St. James

Seize the summits

One important way you can keep moving forward when you would rather turn back is to keep a positive image of success in your mind.

— Pat Williams

Start with a smile
No opera plot can be sensible, for in sensible situations people do not sing.

— Wystan Auden

Focus on what's important
Always a little more.
— John D. Rockefeller, on how much money it takes to satisfy a person

Break the barriers
Character cannot be developed in ease and quiet. Only through experience of trial and suffering can the soul be strengthened, vision cleared, ambition inspired and success achieved.

— Helen Keller

Seize the summits
Pursuing your goals is much like putting together a jigsaw puzzle. While you ultimately seek the final outcome, you still have to work piece by piece. Since you will spend most of your time trying to make progress, you must enjoy what you are doing in order to finish. Take joy from the process, and use the small successes to fuel your continued efforts.

— Dr. David Niven

Start with a smile
I'm in the movie theater, a woman with an enormous head sits down directly in front of the person sitting next to me. I am amused, but only for a few seconds before she changes her mind and sits directly in front of me.

— Rita Rudner

Focus on what's important
An unhurried sense of time is in itself a form of wealth.

— Bonnie Friedman

Break the barriers
It is chiefly through books that we learn from superior minds. In the best books, great men talk to us, give us their most precious thoughts and pour their souls into ours.

— William Channing

Seize the summits
Only by finding your own burning desire will you achieve success.

— Napoleon Hill

Start with a smile

You can learn a lot about paranoids just by following them around.

— *Anonymous*

Focus on what's important

I am happy my teams at UCLA and elsewhere did well and we earned a measure of recognition. But all of that is nothing compared to my family: my wife Nellie, our two children, our seven grandchildren and all ten of our great-grandchildren. All that love is immeasurable.

— *John Wooden*

Break the barriers

Hope is the medicine I use more than any other – hope can cure nearly anything.

— *Dr. McNair Wilson*

Seize the summits

Through perseverance many people win success out of what seemed destined to be certain failure.

— *Benjamin Disraeli*

Start with a smile
Two Americans have been awarded the Nobel Prize for Economics. They are the first to figure out all the charges on their phone bill.

— Jay Leno

Focus on what's important
Blessed are the merciful, for they will be shown mercy.

— Matthew 5:7

Break the barriers
One determined person can make a significant difference, and a small group of determined people can change the course of history.

— Sonia Johnson

Seize the summits
Plans are essential, but I don't think they require religious adherence. If a plan is working, stick with it. If not, change it.

— Robert Dedman

Start with a smile

When a man makes a woman his wife it's the highest compliment he can pay her and it's usually the last.

— Helen Rowland

Focus on what's important

The greatest good we can do for others is not to share our riches but to reveal theirs.

— B.J. Marshall

Break the barriers

I overcame every single one of my personal shortcomings by the sheer passion I brought to my work.

— Sam Walton

Seize the summits

There's no workman, whatsoever he be,
    That may both work well and hastily.

— Chaucer

Start with a smile

That was very important, the wagon. Just as important as wheels are today. Because if the wagon broke down and you were too dumb or lazy to fix it, that's where you stayed. You don't think people headed out for Tulsa, do you? You know, everywhere you see a nice big spread in America, they got two broken wheels outside.

— *Gallagher*

Focus on what's important

Only a life lived for others is a life worthwhile.

— *Albert Einstein*

Break the barriers

I do not try to dance better than anyone else, I only try to dance better than myself.

— *Mikhail Baryshnikov*

Seize the summits

The opportunity of a lifetime is seldom so labeled.

— *American proverb*

Start with a smile
For sincere advice and the correct time, call any number at random at 3:00 am.

— Steve Martin

Focus on what's important
Every time I've done something that doesn't feel right, it ended up not being right.

— Mario Cuomo

Break the barriers
A creative vision gets you going and keeps you going. The very thought of it charges you with energy and fills you with positive feelings. A visionary idea is pregnant not only in its capacity to motivate action but in its capacity to generate additional ideas that support its ultimate realization.

— Laurence Boldt

Seize the summits
Happiness walks on busy feet.

— Kitte Turmell

Start with a smile

Despite the fact that computer speeds are measured in nano-seconds and picoseconds – one billionth and one trillionth of a second, respectively – the smallest interval of time known to man is that which occurs between the traffic light turning green and the driver behind you blowing his horn.

— *Johnny Carson*

Focus on what's important

Smiling conveys self-acceptance and an accepting attitude toward others. It increases others' confidence in themselves and in you. Smiling makes you appear approachable, friendly, relaxed, open and comfortable.

— *Roger Crawford*

Break the barriers

When life's problems seem overwhelming, look around and see what other people are coping with. You may consider yourself fortunate.

— *Ann Landers*

Seize the summits

Where you stumble and fall, there you discover gold.

— *Joseph Campbell*

Start with a smile
Your high school reunion. You get that letter in the mail. You feel like you only have six months to make something of yourself.

— *Drew Carey*

Focus on what's important
Prefer a loss to a dishonest gain, the one brings pain at the moment, the other for all time.

— *Chilon*

Break the barriers
It marks a big step in your development when you come to realize that other people can help you do a better job than you could do alone.

— *Andrew Carnegie*

Seize the summits
Relying on safe choices can sometimes be the enemy of self-esteem, because you're never encouraged to stretch beyond your comfort zone. And if you don't stretch, while you may never fail, you also may never experience the joy of real, hard-earned victory.

— *Francine Ward*

Start with a smile
What makes equality such a difficult business is that we only want it with our superiors.

— *Henry Becque*

Focus on what's important
Kindness has a ripple effect often greater than the act itself. The receiver is happy, surprised and often wakes up to the present moment. When recipients of the kindness tell their stories to others, the kindness extends outward and seeds the idea of being kind in those who hear about it.

— *Susyn Reeve*

Break the barriers
The best time to tackle a minor problem is before it grows up.

— *Hermine Hartley*

Seize the summits
I pray not for victory, but to do my best.

— *Amos Alonzo Stagg*

Start with a smile

Nothing soothes me more after a long and maddening course of piano recitals than to sit and have my teeth drilled.

— *George Bernard Shaw*

Focus on what's important

How much more grievous are the consequences of anger than the causes of it.

— *Marcus Aurelius Antoninus*

Break the barriers

A great part of the information I have was acquired by looking up something and finding something else on the way.

— *Franklin Adams*

Seize the summits

People who make great decisions have a dirty little secret. They make decisions that now and then turn out badly. They make choices that they later see were mistakes. More than you might think. There's no way around this. You can't always make a perfect call on choices that are fraught with uncertainty.

— *Charles Foster*

Start with a smile
Happiness to a dog is what lies on the other side of the door.
— *Charlton Ogburn, Jr.*

Focus on what's important
Luckily, there is a way to be happy. It involves changing the emphasis of our thinking from what we want to what we have. Rather than wishing your spouse were different, try thinking about her wonderful qualities. Instead of complaining about your salary, be grateful that you have a job.
— *Richard Carlson*

Break the barriers
Knowledge is the antidote to fear.
— *Ralph Waldo Emerson*

Seize the summits
We want to perfect ourselves so that we can win with less struggle and increasing ease, but the strange thing is that it's not the easy wins we ostensibly seek but rather the difficult struggles to which we really look forward.
— *Vince Lombardi*

Start with a smile

Trouble turns a man's hair gray in one night. Vanity turns a woman's hair any color in one minute.

— Anonymous

Focus on what's important

An apology is the super glue of life. It can repair almost anything.

— Lynn Johnston

Break the barriers

Showing deference to your boss means that you're loyal and respectful. You'd be amazed how much you can accomplish with a tough boss when you grant him that basic regard.

— Joe Torre

Seize the summits

Be prepared for people to block you and conspire against you. Even your own family may challenge your ability to choose your own way. You can't always expect those close to you to see your dream.

— Les Brown

Start with a smile
I love being married. I was single for a long time, and I just got so sick of finishing my own sentences.

— *Brian Kiley*

Focus on what's important
One of the true signs of respect is when people are loyal to the absent by not speaking behind their backs.

— *Stephen Covey*

Break the barriers
Always try to work for the smartest, brightest, most competent person you can find. If you look at biographies of successful people, it's amazing to find how many crawled up the ladder of success right behind someone else.

— *Al Ries and Jack Trout*

Seize the summits
Fortune favors the adventurous.

— *Desiderius Erasmus*

Start with a smile
A true gentleman is a man who knows how to play the bag-pipes – but doesn't.

— *Anonymous*

Focus on what's important
Real love has staying power. It refuses to look for ways to run away. It always opts for working through.

— *Charles Swindoll*

Break the barriers
Experience has taught me that if I focus predominantly on what I do not have, I am very seldom productive. More often than not, I am frustrated and discouraged. But if I focus only on what I have to work with, I start finding new solutions to old problems.

— *Art Berg*

Seize the summits
The only true happiness comes from squandering ourselves for a purpose.

— *John Mason Brown*

Start with a smile
As Miss America, my goal is to bring peace to the entire world and then to get my own apartment.

— *Jay Leno*

Focus on what's important
You formed us for yourself, and our hearts are restless till they find rest in you.

— *St. Augustine*

Break the barriers
The test of intelligence is not how much we know how to do, but how we behave when we don't know what to do. Similarly, any situation, any activity, that puts before us real problems, that we have to solve for ourselves, problems for which there are no answers in any book, sharpens our intelligence.

— *John Holt*

Seize the summits
Patience and perseverance have a magical effect before which difficulties disappear and obstacles vanish.

— *John Quincy Adams*

Start with a smile

Democracy is a process by which the people are free to choose the man who will get the blame.

— Laurence Peter

Focus on what's important

Tithing – that is, giving 10% of your earnings to the work of God – is one of the best guarantees of prosperity ever known. Many of the world's richest individuals and most successful people have been devout tithers.

— Jack Canfield

Break the barriers

The biggest mistake in life is to think that you work for someone else. True, you may have a boss and you may collect a paycheck from a company but ultimately, you are the master of your own destiny. You decide what potential you reach in your career and what you will eventually accomplish in your life.

— Bob Nelson

Seize the summits

For goals to be useful they need to be specific, otherwise it is difficult to measure whether or not we are achieving them.

— Anthony Grant and Jane Greene

Start with a smile

We've just moved into our dream house. It costs twice as much as we ever dreamed it would.

— *Bob Phillips*

Focus on what's important

Happiness is like a cat. If you try to coax it or call it, it will avoid you. It will never come. But if you pay no attention to it and go about your business, you'll find it rubbing against your legs and jumping into your lap.

— *William Bennett*

Break the barriers

If someone were to ask me what is the most difficult lesson I've learned from being paralyzed, I'm very clear about it: I know I have to give when sometimes I really want to take.

— *Christopher Reeve*

Seize the summits

No man ever progressed to greatness but through great mistakes.

— *Frederick Robertson*

Start with a smile

Please don't talk while I am interrupting.

— Todd Rockefeller

Focus on what's important

Think not because you now are wed
    That all your courtship is at an end.

— Antonio Hurtado de Mendoza

Break the barriers

He who builds to every man's advice will have a crooked house.

— Danish proverb

Seize the summits

No one keeps his enthusiasm automatically. Enthusiasm must be nourished with new actions, new aspiration, new efforts, new vision.

— Papyrus

Start with a smile
When I said "You're a disgrace to mankind," I was talking to myself, not the umpire.

— *John McEnroe*

Focus on what's important
Service isn't a big thing. It's a million little things.

— *Anonymous*

Break the barriers
Avoid the fear of old age by remembering that nothing is ever taken from you without being replaced by something of equal or greater value. Youth, for instance, is replaced by wisdom.

— *Napoleon Hill*

Seize the summits
Setting goals – for both the short term and long term – and going after them is critical to having a successful life. Nearly every decision I made as a young man, and now as an adult, was based on whether or not it moved me closer to my goals.

— *Isiah Thomas*

Start with a smile
A nun alone was a sailboat; two, side by side, a regatta; three, a whole armada. These sisters did not walk; they skimmed, they hovered.
— *Richard Selzer, on Sisters of Mercy in full habit*

Focus on what's important
Beware of the barrenness of an overcrowded life.
— *John Maxwell*

Break the barriers
In every crisis there is a message. Crises are nature's way of forcing change – breaking down old structures, shaking loose negative habits so that something new and better can take their place.
— *Susan Taylor*

Seize the summits
I never cease to be amazed by how many times I've achieved results simply because I took the trouble (and, in many cases, had the gall or audacity) to ask – and kept asking until I got the yes I was after.
— *Robert Ringer*

Start with a smile
Nothing tastes better than the stuff you're eating when you're cheating on your diet.

— Anonymous

Focus on what's important
Everyone should have a deep-seated interest or hobby to enrich his mind, add zest to living and perhaps, depending upon what it is, result in a service to his country.

— Dale Carnegie

Break the barriers
Cultivation to the mind is as necessary as food to the body.

— Cicero

Seize the summits
Folks who never do any more than they get paid for, never get paid for any more than they do.

— Elbert Hubbard

Start with a smile

To keep a true perspective of your importance, you should have a dog that will worship you and a cat that will ignore you.

— *Rita Kubran*

Focus on what's important

The ultimate test of man's conscience may be his willingness to sacrifice something today for future generations whose words of thanks will not be heard.

— *Gaylord Nelson*

Break the barriers

The one thing that will guarantee the successful conclusion of a doubtful undertaking is faith that you can do it.

— *William James*

Seize the summits

No one has time; we have to make time.

— *James Rhoen*

Start with a smile
Boot: A shallow puddle worn on the foot.
— *Henry Beard and Roy McKie*

Focus on what's important
We must beware of packing our schedules by saying "yes" to things which mean "no" to our families. Now is the time to take time. There is no other.
— *R. Kent Hughes*

Break the barriers
A lasting work requires extensive preparation.
— *Douglas Rumford*

Seize the summits
By itself, no goal is compelling. No matter how good the idea, no one will go through the inevitable – and often painful – ups and downs of making it happen unless they really care. Those who reach their goals must have a passion driving them, a personal fervor.
— *Marilyn Tam*

Start with a smile
The murals in restaurants are about on a par with the food in art galleries.

— Peter DeVries

Focus on what's important
Establishing goals is all right if you don't let them deprive you of interesting detours.

— Doug Larson

Break the barriers
I don't think of myself as a poor deprived ghetto girl who made good. I think of myself as somebody who from an early age knew I was responsible for myself, and I had to make good.

— Oprah Winfrey

Seize the summits
Vision is the art of seeing things invisible.

— Jonathan Swift

Start with a smile

It takes real talent to be able to apologize in a manner that makes the offended person feel guilty.

— Anonymous

Focus on what's important

Use soft words in hard arguments.

— Henry Bohn

Break the barriers

It is a good thing to read books of quotations. When engraved upon the memory, quotations give you good thoughts.

— Sir Winston Churchill

Seize the summits

Remember that what is hard to endure will be sweet to recall.

— Tote Yamada

Start with a smile
The best way to avoid ballplayers is to go to a good restaurant.
— *Tim McCarver*

Focus on what's important
Fame is a vapor, popularity is an accident, money takes wings, those who cheer you today may curse you tomorrow. The only thing that endures is character.
— *Horace Greeley*

Break the barriers
Get a lot of sunlight.
— *John D. Rockefeller, Jr.*

Seize the summits
People are more easily led than driven.
— *David Fink*

Start with a smile

Housework is a treadmill from futility to oblivion with stop-offs at tedium and counter-productivity.

— *Erma Bombeck*

Focus on what's important

Success can also cause misery. The trick is not to be surprised when you discover it doesn't bring you all the happiness and answers you thought it would.

— *Prince*

Break the barriers

One great technique to deal with your fears in the face of adversity is to recount past challenges that you have successfully overcome. Your ability to manage present circumstances is improved when you recall past fears that were never ultimately realized.

— *Art Berg*

Seize the summits

The slow penny is surer than the quick dollar. The slow trotter will out-travel the fleet racer. Genius darts, flutters and tires; but perseverance wears and wins.

— *Orison Marden*

Start with a smile
Bagel: A doughnut dipped in cement.

— Anonymous

Focus on what's important
It's important to know that at the end of the day it's not the medals you remember. What you remember is the process – what you learn about yourself by challenging yourself, the experiences you share with other people, the honesty the training demands – those are things nobody can take away from you whether you finish twelfth or you're an Olympic champion.

— Silken Laumann

Break the barriers
Worry – a god, invisible but omnipotent. It steals the bloom from the cheek and lightness from the pulse; it takes away the appetite, and turns the hair grey.

— Benjamin Disraeli

Seize the summits
The most successful men have used seeming failures as stepping stones to better things.

— Greenville Kleiser

Start with a smile

Remember – a developer is someone who wants to build a house in the woods. An environmentalist is someone who already owns a house in the woods.

— Dennis Miller

Focus on what's important

Relationships will fluctuate with the ups and downs through the stages and ages of life. If you bail out when things are down, you will regret it once you are out.

— T.D. Jakes

Break the barriers

Self-esteem isn't everything; it's just that there's nothing without it.

— Gloria Steinem

Seize the summits

Man cannot discover new oceans unless he has the courage to lose sight of the shore.

— André Gide

Start with a smile

Phone conversations are over in 30 seconds flat.

— Anonymous, on why it's great to be a man

Focus on what's important

Reprove your friends in secret, praise them openly.

— Publilius Syrus

Break the barriers

A problem clearly stated is a problem half solved.

— Dorthea Brande

Seize the summits

My level of excitement and drive comes from my goals. Every morning when I wake up, even if I feel physically exhausted from a lack of sleep, I'll still find the drive I need because my goals are so exciting to me. They get me up early, keep me up late and inspire me to marshal my resources and use everything I can possibly find within the sphere of my influence to accomplish them.

— Anthony Robbins

Start with a smile
The main advantage of being famous is that when you bore people at dinner parties they think it is their fault.

— *Henry Kissinger*

Focus on what's important
After more than sixty years of almost daily reading of the Bible, I never fail to find it always new and marvelously in tune with the changing needs of every day.

— *Cecil B. DeMille*

Break the barriers
Don't let yesterday use up too much of today.

— *Will Rogers*

Seize the summits
Some objectives are clearly more critical than others. We must learn to distinguish between what is "merely important" and what is "wildly important." A "wildly important goal" carries serious consequences. Failure to achieve these goals renders all other achievements relatively inconsequential.

— *Stephen Covey*

Start with a smile
It is the responsibility of the man to ask for the date, and the responsibility of the woman to think up excuses that get progressively more obvious until the man figures out that the woman would rather chew on a rat pancreas.

— Dave Barry

Focus on what's important
He who always listens to what other people say about him will never find inner peace.

— Leo Tolstoy

Break the barriers
The change of one simple behavior can affect other behaviors and thus change many things.

— Jean Baer

Seize the summits
If you set a goal it is impossible to be a total failure, at least you have succeeded in taking command of your own destiny.

— Robert Schuller

Start with a smile

The most important thing in acting is honesty. If you can fake that, you've got it made.

— George Burns

Focus on what's important

Give, and it will be given to you. A good measure, pressed down, shaken together and running over, will be poured into your lap. For with the measure you use, it will be measured to you.

— Luke 6:38

Break the barriers

He that is discontented in one place will seldom be content in another.

— Aesop

Seize the summits

A champion pays an extra price to be better than everybody else.

— Bear Bryant

Start with a smile

An amateur is a young man who, when flattering women, is afraid of overdoing it.

— Anonymous

Focus on what's important

People who enjoy what they are doing invariably do it well.

— Joe Gibbs

Break the barriers

We tend to think that it is being unhappy that leads people to complain, when actually it is complaining that leads people to become unhappy.

— Joan Lunden

Seize the summits

Nothing shapes your life more than the commitments you choose to make. Your commitments can develop you or they can destroy you, but either way, they will define you. Tell me what you are committed to, and I'll tell you what you will be in twenty years. We become whatever we are committed to.

— Rick Warren

Start with a smile
If you really want to irritate a stewardess, when she asks you to put your seat in an upright position, stand on your head.

— *Robert Orben*

Focus on what's important
Abundance consists not so much in material possessions, but in an uncovetous spirit.

— *John Selden*

Break the barriers
Every young person should have a mentor. Students, business-people, even ballplayers. They need wisdom and experience. They need encouragement. They need someone who has been through it all.

— *Yogi Berra*

Seize the summits
Success demands singleness of purpose.

— *Vince Lombardi*

Start with a smile

An egotist is a person of low taste, more interested in himself than in me.

— *Ambrose Bierce*

Focus on what's important

I have the feeling when I write poetry that I'm doing what I'm supposed to do. You don't think about whether you're going to get money or fame, you just do it.

— *Doris Lund*

Break the barriers

I thank God for my handicaps for, through them, I have found myself, my work and my God.

— *Helen Keller*

Seize the summits

Ah, but a man's reach should exceed his grasp, Or what's a heaven for?

— *Robert Browning*

Start with a smile
Those who resemble us we find good-looking, well set up, and above all charming.

— *Jean de la Fontaine*

Focus on what's important
By continuously engaging a cycle of longing, you never actually allow yourself to be in the present. You end up living your life at some point just off in the future. You only have one moment – the one right here, right now. If you skip over "here" in your rush to get "there," you deny yourself the full range of feelings and sensations that can only be experienced in the present moment.

— *Cherie Carter-Scott*

Break the barriers
A successful man is one who can lay a firm foundation with bricks that others throw at him.

— *David Brinkley*

Seize the summits
Doing the best you are capable of doing is victory in itself, and less than that is defeat.

— *John Wooden*

Start with a smile
Whenever you hear the word *save,* it is usually the beginning of an advertisement designed to make you spend money.

— *Anonymous*

Focus on what's important
God grant me the courage not to give up what I think is right, even though I think it is hopeless.

— *Admiral Chester Nimitz*

Break the barriers
When you can't trace God's hand, trust his heart.

— *Max Lucado*

Seize the summits
Expanding your comfort zone makes you feel good about yourself.

— *Richard Templar*

Start with a smile
Men do cry, but only when assembling furniture.

— *Rita Rudner*

Focus on what's important
Love is the willingness to accept another person with all of his or her faults and limitations, and to be infinitely grateful that this other person accepts you with all of yours.

— *Rabbi Harold Kushner*

Break the barriers
Deep faith eliminates fear.

— *Lech Walesa*

Seize the summits
You have to have goals – singular ones and long-range ones. I wanted to make the Olympic team badly, and it only took me 12 years of training to do it. If you're crazy enough, obstinate enough, dedicated enough, you can do almost anything. You just need the courage and patience to stay with it.

— *Phil Mulkey*

Start with a smile
Psychologists: A man who, when a voluptuous girl enters a room, watches the other men's reactions.

— *Anonymous*

Focus on what's important
It's not what you earn that makes you wealthy or financially secure, it's what you save.

— *Peter Lowe*

Break the barriers
I have to remember to tell the negative committee that meets in my head to sit down and shut up.

— *Kathy Kendall*

Seize the summits
For decisions whose ramifications are minimal or can easily be rescinded, be quick and decisive. For decisions that have greater effects or can't be reversed, devote more time to careful study.

— *Tom Gegax*

Start with a smile

Memory is a marvelous thing – it enables you to remember a mistake each time you repeat it.

— *Max Kauffmann*

Focus on what's important

While forbidden fruit is said to taste sweeter, it usually spoils faster.

— *Abigail Van Buren*

Break the barriers

The one way to get thin is to reestablish a purpose in life. Obesity is often a mental state, a disease brought on by boredom and disappointment.

— *Cyril Connolly*

Seize the summits

With them I gladly shared my all and learned the great truth that where God guides, He provides.

— *Franklin Buchman*

❧ June 4

Start with a smile
When we grandchildren were all gathered around the dinner table bored out of our minds, when no other adult was watching, eyes twinkling my grandmother would quietly detach her upper bridge and roll it out on her tongue with three tiny false teeth riding on it, and as our eyes bugged out, we could hear her characteristic deep delighted chuckle.

— Susan Kenney

Focus on what's important
Polite words open iron gates.

— Serbo-Croatian proverb

Break the barriers
Every noble work is at first impossible.

— Thomas Carlyle

Seize the summits
Never despair; but if you do, work on in despair.

— Terence

Start with a smile

I'm against picketing, but I don't know how to show it.

— *Mitch Hedberg*

Focus on what's important

Humility leads to strength and not to weakness. It is the highest form of self-respect to admit mistakes and to make amends for them.

— *John McCloy*

Break the barriers

When we are fatigued, our resistance is down. We make poorer decisions. We are more fearful. We cannot handle stress as well. We don't feel as well, and we are much less likely to expect positive results. This is why all the military services emphasize physical fitness for everyone, whether your job is that of an office clerk, or a Navy Seal, or an Army Ranger.

— *Major William Cohen*

Seize the summits

Good merchandise, even when hidden, soon finds buyers.

— *Plautus*

June 6

Start with a smile
According to *Modern Bride* magazine, the average bride spends 150 hours planning her wedding. The average groom spends 150 hours going, "Yeah, sounds good."

— *Jay Leno*

Focus on what's important
When the truth is in your way, you are on the wrong road.

— *Josh Billings*

Break the barriers
Anyone who stops learning is old, whether at twenty or eighty. Anyone who keeps learning stays young.

— *Henry Ford*

Seize the summits
Don't wait until you feel like taking a positive action. Take the action and then you will feel like doing it.

— *Zig Ziglar*

Start with a smile

A modern computer is an electronic wonder that performs complex mathematical calculations and intricate accounting tabulations in one ten-thousandth of a second – and then mails out statements ten days later.

— Paul Sweeney

Focus on what's important

Laughter is the shortest distance between two people.

— Victor Borge

Break the barriers

Communication is less about speaking than about listening.

— Rick Pitino

Seize the summits

To climb steep hills requires a slow pace at first.

— William Shakespeare

Start with a smile
My wife called me. She said, "There's water in the carburetor." I said, "Where's the car?" She said, "In the lake."

— *Henny Youngman*

Focus on what's important
Feeling down, we often forget to look up. Then the more we ignore wonders large and small, the lower we feel. And yet, it is nearly impossible to catch a glimpse of a newborn child, a goldfinch feeding on thistle, or a bright red sun in the sky and not feel part of something magnificent.

— *Dr. Suzanne Zoglio*

Break the barriers
Trouble knocked at the door, but hearing a laugh within, hurried away.

— *Benjamin Franklin*

Seize the summits
Your capacity to say no determines your capability to say yes to greater things.

— *E. Stanley Jones*

Start with a smile

Guest towel: A small square of non-absorbent fabric surrounded by waterproof embroidery.

— *Anonymous*

Focus on what's important

Charity is the bone shared with the dog when you are just as hungry as the dog.

— *Jack London*

Break the barriers

Nature arms each man with some faculty which enables him to do easily some feat impossible to any other.

— *Ralph Waldo Emerson*

Seize the summits

Dreams come a size too big so that we can grow into them.

— *Josie Bisset*

Start with a smile
The trouble with women is that they never put the toilet seat back up.

— *Simon Nye*

Focus on what's important
The power of reconciliation is stronger than revenge. It is amazing how forgiveness unloads the weapon in the other person's hand.

— *Charles Swindoll*

Break the barriers
Discover someone to help shoulder your misfortunes. Then you will never be alone. Neither fate, nor the crowd, so readily attacks two.

— *Baltasar Gracián*

Seize the summits
They never raised a statue to a critic.

— *Martha Graham*

Start with a smile
A thousand dollars invested at just 8% for 400 years grows to $23 quadrillion. But the first 100 years are the hardest.

— Sidney Homer

Focus on what's important
To keep your marriage brimming,
    With love in the loving cup,
    When you're wrong, admit it.
    When you're right, shut up.

— Ogden Nash

Break the barriers
Employ your times in improving yourself by other men's writings so that you shall come easily by what others have labored hard for.

— Socrates

Seize the summits
If there's one characteristic all winners share, it's that they care more than anyone else. No detail is too small to sweat or too large to dream.

— Jack Welch

Start with a smile

Just after my thirtieth birthday, instead of growing hair on my head, I now was growing it in places where I didn't need it, like the top of my ear. A strand had sprouted there overnight and made me look like something out of *The Cat in the Hat*.

— *Bill Cosby*

Focus on what's important

True happiness doesn't come from "things." It comes from love. Love of God, family, friends, strangers and self.

— *Jeff Foxworthy*

Break the barriers

The best promoter of health is something to do.

— *John Burroughs*

Seize the summits

Successful people are willing to engage in drudgery in the cause of something marvelous. The greater part of genius is the years of effort invested to solve a problem or find the perfect expression of an idea. With hard work you acquire knowledge about yourself that idleness never reveals.

— *Tom Butler-Bowdon*

Start with a smile

Before I speak, I have something important to say.

— *Groucho Marx*

Focus on what's important

He that will make good use of any part of his life must allow a large part of it to recreation.

— *John Locke*

Break the barriers

Staying calm is the best way to take the wind out of an angry person's sails.

— *Anonymous*

Seize the summits

Do not listen to yourself when the little voice of fear inside of you rears its ugly head and says, "They are all smarter than you out there. They are more talented, they are taller, blonder, prettier, luckier and have connections. They have a cousin who took out Meryl Streep's baby-sitter." Give credence at all to that voice, and your worst fears will surely come true.

— *Neil Simon*

Start with a smile
Dust is a protective coating for the furniture.

— *Mario Buatta*

Focus on what's important
If you begin with prayer, you can think more clearly and make fewer stupid mistakes.

— *Sir John Templeton*

Break the barriers
We who lived in concentration camps can remember the men who walked through the huts comforting others, giving away their last piece of bread. They offer sufficient proof that everything can be taken from a man but one thing: the last of the human freedoms – to choose one's attitude in any given set of circumstances.

— *Viktor Frankl*

Seize the summits
Accomplish the great task by a series of small acts.

— *Lao Tzu*

Start with a smile
When a man and woman marry they become one. The trouble starts when they try to decide which one.

— *Anonymous*

Focus on what's important
If I'm such a legend, why am I so lonely?

— *Judy Garland*

Break the barriers
When one door closes another door opens; but we so often look so long and so regretfully upon the closed door, that we do not see the ones which open for us.

— *Alexander Graham Bell*

Seize the summits
I have not failed. I've just found 10,000 ways that don't work.

— *Thomas Edison*

Start with a smile

"We must do lunch sometime" is the polite euphemism for, "I don't care if I never see you again."

— *Marcus Hunt*

Focus on what's important

Every job has drudgery, whether it is in the home, in the professional school or in the office. The first secret of happiness is the recognition of this fundamental fact.

— *Millicent McIntosh*

Break the barriers

It is never too late to be what you might have been.

— *George Elliot*

Seize the summits

You want to set a goal that is big enough that in the process of achieving it you become someone worth becoming.

— *Jim Hohn*

Start with a smile

I've never understood why women love cats. Cats are independent, they don't listen, they don't come in when you call, they like to stay out all night, and when they're home they like to be left alone and sleep. In other words, every quality that women hate in a man, they love in a cat.

— Jay Leno

Focus on what's important

To give help when it is asked for is friendship. To give appropriate help before it is asked for is love.

— Dr. Theodore Rubin

Break the barriers

Control what you can, let go of the rest.

— Joe Torre

Seize the summits

No good comes from hurrying.

— Jewish proverb

Start with a smile
Farm: What a city man dreams of at 5 p.m., never at 5 a.m.

— *Anonymous*

Focus on what's important
To get nowhere, follow the crowd.

— *Frank Baer*

Break the barriers
The man who puts $10,000 additional capital into an established business is pretty certain of increased returns; and in the same way, the man who puts additional capital into his brains – information – will as surely get increased returns. There is no capital and no increase in capital safer than that.

— *Marshall Field*

Seize the summits
Often we are caught in a mental trap of seeing enormously successful people and thinking they are where they are because they have some special gift. Yet a closer look shows that the greatest gift that extraordinarily successful people have over the average person is their ability to get themselves to take action.

— *Anthony Robbins*

Start with a smile

Take time when reading a map: When your partner is driving along an interstate, wait until the car has just passed the correct exit before stating firmly, "That was the right one."

— *Craig Brown*

Focus on what's important

Music washes away from the soul the dust of everyday life.

— *Berthold Auerbach*

Break the barriers

When my life is in order, I have more time to work on constructive, long-term projects, not to mention more time for pleasurable activities. The more one maintains a daily routine, the less his mind is clogged with petty problems, which, in turn, translates into lower stress and anxiety.

— *Robert Ringer*

Seize the summits

The secret to persevering is building your self-esteem so you can take rejection and move on to the next opportunity.

— *Jack Canfield*

Start with a smile

It's easy to find reasons why other folks should be patient.

— *George Eliot*

Focus on what's important

Of all the things you wear, your expression is the most important.

— *Janet Lane*

Break the barriers

"How do you know so much about everything?" was asked of a wise and intelligent man; and the answer was "By never being afraid or ashamed to ask questions as to anything of which I was ignorant."

— *John Abbott*

Seize the summits

Get your major purpose clear, take off your plate all which hinders that purpose and hold hard to all that helps it, and then go ahead with a clear conscience, courage, sincerity and selflessness.

— *Field Marshall Bernard Montgomery*

Start with a smile

Loser: A lightning rod salesman who gets caught outside in a storm with a handful of samples.

— Anonymous

Focus on what's important

Cheerfulness and content are great beautifiers and famous preservers of youthful looks.

— Charles Dickens

Break the barriers

If you would not have affliction visit you twice, listen at once to what it teaches.

— James Burgh

Seize the summits

Years may wrinkle the skin, but to give up interest wrinkles the soul.

— General Douglas MacArthur

Start with a smile

I took a speed-reading course where you run your finger down the middle of the page and was able to read War and Peace in twenty minutes. It's about Russia.

— *Woody Allen*

Focus on what's important

No one who smiles is homely.

— *Robert Half*

Break the barriers

The growth of wisdom may be gauged accurately by the decline of ill temper.

— *Friedrich Nietzsche*

Seize the summits

You may not accomplish every goal you set – no one does – but what really matters is having goals and going after them whole-heartedly. In the end, it is the person you become, not the things you achieve, that is most important.

— *Les Brown*

Start with a smile
The nice thing about egoists is that they don't talk about other people.

— *Lucille Harper*

Focus on what's important
Simple gifts such as a compliment, a note, a telephone call or a simple act of kindness – these are the truest forms of giving because they come from the heart – they are literally a portion of the giver.

— *David Dunn*

Break the barriers
People make decisions about you and your ideas based on what they see – your facial expression, your body language and your enthusiasm. So if you want to communicate confidence and strength, and sell your idea, start by being enthusiastic.

— *Joan Lunden*

Seize the summits
Those who attain any excellence, commonly spend life in one pursuit; for excellence is not often gained upon easier terms.

— *Samuel Johnson*

Start with a smile

We all have strength enough to endure the misfortune of others.

— *François de La Rochefoucauld*

Focus on what's important

You can easily judge the character of a man by how he treats those who can do nothing for him.

— *James Miles*

Break the barriers

A severely impaired person never knows his hidden strength until he is treated like a normal human being and encouraged to try to shape his own life. Annie Sullivan regarded the blind as human beings endowed with rights to education, recreation and employment, and she strove to arrange my life accordingly. Teacher believed in me, and I resolved not to betray her faith.

— *Helen Keller*

Seize the summits

Life shrinks or expands in proportion to one's courage.

— *Anaïs Nin*

Start with a smile

My days of having hair are numbered. The once-bustling down-town of my abundantly populated scalp is becoming a wasteland of burned-out storefronts and boarded-up windows as the occu-pants move to the outlying suburbs of my neck, ears and back.

— *Dennis Miller*

Focus on what's important

If you find that you are not feeling in love anymore, be more loving.

— *Frank Pittman III*

Break the barriers

Jimmy taught me a long time ago that you do the best you can and don't worry about the criticisms. Once you accept the fact that you're not perfect, then you develop some confidence.

— *Rosalynn Carter*

Seize the summits

What keeps me going is goals.

— *Muhammad Ali*

Start with a smile

Banks will lend you money if you can prove you don't need it.

— *Mark Twain*

Focus on what's important

There are few things in life that equal the sensation of being paid up.

— *Kin Hubbard*

Break the barriers

Keep your faith in all beautiful things; in the sun when it is hidden, in the spring when it is gone.

— *Roy Gibson*

Seize the summits

If you can meet success and failure and treat them both as imposters, then you are a balanced man, my son.

— *Rudyard Kipling*

Start with a smile
Men seem to flip around the television more than women. Women will stop and go, "Well let me see what the show is before I change the channel. Maybe we can nurture it, work with it, help it grow into something." Men don't do that. Because women nest and men hunt.

— *Jerry Seinfeld*

Focus on what's important
Do not speak evil about the ruler of your people.

— *Acts 23:5*

Break the barriers
The first degree of folly is to conceit one's self wise; the second to profess it; the third to despise counsel.

— *Benjamin Franklin*

Seize the summits
One who doesn't try cannot fail and become wise.

— *William Saroyan*

◈ June 28

Start with a smile
No matter how busy people are, they are never too busy to stop and talk about how busy they are.

— Anonymous

Focus on what's important
Grumbling is the death of love.

— Marlene Dietrich

Break the barriers
All the adversity I've had in my life, all my troubles and obstacles, have strengthened me. You may not realize it when it happens, but a kick in the teeth may be the best thing in the world for you.

— Walt Disney

Seize the summits
That which we persist in doing becomes easier for us to do. Not that the nature of the thing has changed, but our power to do has increased.

— Heber Grant

Start with a smile

Most people work up the courage to ask for a raise by remembering that it takes less nerve to ask for the increase than it does to go home and tell your spouse that you couldn't work up the nerve.

— *Gene Perret*

Focus on what's important

Do not lose your peace of mind over unimportant matters. Life is too precious to be sacrificed for the nonessential and transient. Ignore the inconsequential.

— *Grenville Kleiser*

Break the barriers

He has good judgment who doesn't rely wholly on his own.

— *Thomas Fuller*

Seize the summits

The work will teach you how to do it.

— *Estonian proverb*

Start with a smile
Live within your income, even if you have to borrow to do it.
— *Josh Billings*

Focus on what's important
The first step in changing or improving another is to accept him as he is. Nothing reinforces defensive behavior more than judgment, comparison or rejection. A feeling of acceptance and worth frees a person from the need to defend and helps release the natural growth tendency to improve.
— *Stephen Covey*

Break the barriers
Those who are successful are those who have known more than the average person considers necessary.
— *F.D. Van Ambergh*

Seize the summits
A professional is one who does his best work when he feels the least like working.
— *Frank Lloyd Wright*

Start with a smile

My husband is so confident that when he watches sports on television, he thinks that if he concentrates he can help his team. If the team is in trouble, he coaches the players from our living room, and if they're really in trouble, I have to get off the phone in case they call him.

— Rita Rudner

Focus on what's important

It is better to fail in originality than to succeed in imitation.

— Herman Melville

Break the barriers

There is healing power in laughter. It makes us forget, makes us relax and makes us feel like life is worth living again.

— Art Berg

Seize the summits

The bottom line with scheduling is this: when you commit yourself to writing down things to do that support your desires, which in turn support your life's mission, you increase the likelihood that you'll be able to avoid being sidetracked.

— Tom Gegax

Start with a smile
My doctor recently told me that jogging could add years to my life. I think he was right. I feel ten years older already.

— *Milton Berle*

Focus on what's important
Risk more than others think is safe. Care more than others think is wise. Dream more than others think is practical. Expect more than others think is possible.

— *U.S. Military Academy cadet maxim*

Break the barriers
What I hear, I forget; what I see, I remember; what I do, I understand.

— *Confucius*

Seize the summits
A thoroughbred horse never looks at the other horses. It just concentrates on running the fastest race it can.

— *Henry Fonda*

Start with a smile

My decision is maybe . . . and that's final!

— *Sign on a businessman's desk*

Focus on what's important

Let us be servants in order to be leaders.

— *Fyodor Dostoevsky*

Break the barriers

Select the person who, in your opinion, is the finest person in all the world, past or present. Make him or her your pacesetter for the rest of your life, emulating him or her in every possible way.

— *Napoleon Hill*

Seize the summits

Dreams are where we want to end up. Goals are how we get there. Dreams are our vision of where we are after our struggle, the prize at the end of the journey. Goals are the individual steps we take to ultimately deserve the prize.

— *Rick Pitino*

Start with a smile

G.K. Chesterton was once asked what single book he would most like to have if he were stranded on a desert island. With typical wit, he replied, *Thomas' Guide to Practical Shipbuilding.*

— *Bruce Larson*

Focus on what's important

Effective listening is more than simply avoiding the bad habit of interrupting others while they are speaking or finishing their sentences. It's being content to listen to the entire thought of someone rather than waiting impatiently for your chance to respond.

— *Richard Carlson*

Break the barriers

The ability to prepare to win is as important as the will to win.

— *Bobby Knight*

Seize the summits

We will always have time for the things we put first.

— *Liane Steele*

Start with a smile

Solutide: The state of being closer to nature than to the nearest flush toilet.

— Henry Beard and Roy McKie

Focus on what's important

Kind words can be short and easy to speak but their echoes are truly endless.

— Mother Teresa

Break the barriers

The most interesting thing about cancer is that it can be one of the most positive, life-affirming, incredible experiences ever. When somebody is in that position, he starts to really focus on his life, on his friends and family, and what's really important.

— Lance Armstrong

Seize the summits

Define success in terms of how well you honor your commitment to the process.

— Dr. Bob Rotella

Start with a smile
With enough inside information and a million dollars, you can go broke in a year.

— *Warren Buffett*

Focus on what's important
If you are having trouble pursuing your passion, you can still find real happiness by putting passion into your current pursuits. Each of us can find our calling where we are, right now, if we only begin to see the higher purpose to our task. The farmer provides nourishment, the builder gives shelter, the office worker offers assistance and solves problems for customers and fellow workers.

— *Thomas Kinkade*

Break the barriers
Trust your hopes, not your fears.

— *David Mahoney*

Seize the summits
Don't succumb to excuses. Go back to the job of making the corrections and forming the habits that will make your goal possible.

— *Vince Lombardi*

Start with a smile

Inflation: What used to cost 20 dollars to buy now costs 40 dollars to repair.

— *Anonymous*

Focus on what's important

The man who keeps busy helping the man below him won't have time to envy the man above him.

— *Henrietta Mears*

Break the barriers

Maintain an attitude of unconditional self-worth, free from self-criticism. You can agree that it is cruel and unnecessary to tell someone else, "You are really stupid – what a klutz – you should give up – you keep making the same mistakes – you'll never be any good!" If you would never say those things to anyone else, why not pay yourself the same courtesy?

— *Dan Millman*

Seize the summits

Do few things but do them well; simple joys are holy.

— *St. Francis of Assisi*

Start with a smile

You can say any foolish thing to a dog, and the dog will give you a look that says, "Wow, you're right! I never would've thought of that!"

— Dave Barry

Focus on what's important

To be independent of public opinion is the first formal condition of achieving anything great.

— George Hegel

Break the barriers

I not only use all the brains I have, but all I can borrow.

— Woodrow Wilson

Seize the summits

It's easier for the mind to accept a small piece than a big chunk that appears too hard to handle. So reduce all tasks into smaller, more manageable pieces and then do something. Take some action regardless of how small. It's better to do something than nothing at all. Once you get moving, it's amazing how the next action will follow.

— Francine Ward

Start with a smile
The IRS sent back my tax return saying I owed eight hundred dollars. I said, "If you'll notice, I sent a paper clip with my return. Given what you've been paying for things lately, that should more than make up the difference."

— *Emo Philips*

Focus on what's important
In lovers' quarrels, the party that loves most is always most willing to acknowledge the greater fault.

— *Sir Walter Scott*

Break the barriers
What we do upon some occasion will probably depend on what we already are; and what we already are will be the result of previous years of self-discipline.

— *Vince Lombardi*

Seize the summits
The harder you work, the more luck you have.

— *Dave Thomas*

Start with a smile

When a woman tries on clothing from her closet that feels tight, she will assume she has gained weight. When a man tries on clothing from his closet that feels tight, he will assume the clothing has shrunk.

— Rita Rudner

Focus on what's important

Replace the quick shower with the long soak. Warm baths can lower your blood pressure, expand the vessels throughout your body and around your heart and provide a place to get away from it all. Take a leisurely warm bath with the lights out and practice ignoring the pestering of your hyperactive brain.

— Dr. Paul Pearsall

Break the barriers

I pray hard, work hard and leave the rest to God.

— Florence Griffith Joyner

Seize the summits

Action is the antidote to despair.

— Joan Baez

Start with a smile

Whenever I start to think the world is moving too fast, I go to the Post Office.

— Billy Connolly

Focus on what's important

We treat strangers exceedingly well and usually reserve our best attentions for people we work with. Our partner gets missed, lost in the bustle of it all. In fact, we should treat them better than anyone else. After all, they are supposed to be the most important person in the world to us.

— Richard Templar

Break the barriers

Nothing splendid has ever been achieved except for those who dare to believe that something inside of them was superior to circumstance.

— Bruce Barton

Seize the summits

If you're big enough for your dream, your dream isn't big enough for you.

— Erwin McManus

~ July 12

Start with a smile
A man I know solved the problem of too many visiting relatives. He borrowed money from the rich ones and loaned it to the poor ones. Now none of them come back.

— *Bob Phillips*

Focus on what's important
If you really love one another, you will not be able to avoid making sacrifices.

— *Mother Teresa*

Break the barriers
Any nagging self-doubts about being over the hill or under-skilled tend to fade in proportion to the amount of new information we acquire. A work in progress is full of potential. Keep learning and you'll always be self-assured.

— *Dr. Suzanne Zoglio*

Seize the summits
Anyone who proposes to do good must not expect people to roll stones out of his way, but must accept his lot calmly even if they roll a few more upon it.

— *Albert Schweitzer*

Start with a smile
You got to have smelt a lot of mule manure before you can sing like a hillbilly.

— Hank Williams

Focus on what's important
The places of rest that we carve out for ourselves are often where we best assess our life, our dreams, our heartaches, our faith. The power of rest is that it allows us to enjoy the journey of life, not just the destination.

— T.D. Jakes

Break the barriers
Speak properly, and in as few words as you can, but always plainly; for the end of speech is not ostentation, but to be understood.

— William Penn

Seize the summits
It's a nice thought that old age is always ten years older than you are now, but it can lead to postponing the future till you end up as the man with a bright future behind him. Whatever happened to old so-and-so?

— Charles Handy

Start with a smile
A genius is one who can do anything except make a living.
— *Joey Adams*

Focus on what's important
True happiness is not attained through self-gratification, but through fidelity to a worthy purpose.
— *Helen Keller*

Break the barriers
When you face your fear, most of the time you will discover that it was not really such a big threat after all.
— *Les Brown*

Seize the summits
It is not the critic who counts. The credit belongs to the man who is actually in the arena; whose face is marred with sweat and dust and blood; who strives valiantly; who errs and comes short again and again; who knows the great enthusiasms, the great devotions and spends himself in a worthy cause and who, if he fails, at least fails while bearing greatly so that his place shall never be with those cold and timid souls who know neither victory nor defeat.
— *Theodore Roosevelt*

Start with a smile

The thing which in the subway is called congestion is highly esteemed in the night spots.

— Simeon Strunsky

Focus on what's important

Paraplegics and lottery winners do not differ significantly in their degree of reported happiness. If you will cease comparing yourself and your success with others and learn to attend more fully to the simple joyful moments of life, you are more likely to feel sweetly successful.

— Dr. Paul Pearsall

Break the barriers

I don't think I could have been so successful if I didn't have faith in a higher being. There are times when I get so tired. But with God, I know something bigger is driving me, I can do anything.

— Claire Prymus

Seize the summits

To avoid drifting away from your focus, ask yourself at regular intervals, "Is what I'm doing right now helping me to achieve my goals?" That takes practice.

— Jack Canfield and Mark Victor Hansen

Start with a smile

There are three ways to get something done: do it yourself, employ someone or forbid your children to do it.

— *Monta Crane*

Focus on what's important

Be the first to say sorry. Saying sorry has many benefits, even if it does stick in your throat a little. Not only does it give you the moral advantage, but it also diffuses tension, gets rid of bad feelings and clears the air. Chances are that if you say sorry first, they will probably be humbled into apologizing also.

— *Richard Templar*

Break the barriers

Walking is man's best medicine.

— *Hippocrates*

Seize the summits

The difference between a successful person and others is not a lack of strength, not a lack of knowledge, but rather a lack of will.

— *Vince Lombardi*

Start with a smile

A lot of people become pessimists from financing optimists.

— *C.T. Jones*

Focus on what's important

Life is a paradise for those who love many things with a passion.

— *Leo Buscaglia*

Break the barriers

It is a common experience that a problem difficult at night is resolved in the morning after the committee of sleep has worked on it.

— *John Steinbeck*

Seize the summits

When I have a cause I'm committed to, achieving it becomes much more important to me than the obstacles in the way.

— *Marilyn Tam*

Start with a smile
There are a handful of people whom money won't spoil, and we all count ourselves among them.

— *Mignon McLaughlin*

Focus on what's important
To be humble to superiors is duty, to equals courtesy, to inferiors nobleness.

— *Benjamin Franklin*

Break the barriers
The real irony is this: some of the happiest, most joy-filled people I know are people who have been through some of the worst pain in the world. I don't know exactly why that happens, but this is my guess: once we're no longer afraid to feel any feeling that comes our way, we really do become happy, joyous and free.

— *Melody Beattie*

Seize the summits
Decide what your priorities are and how much time you'll spend on them. If you don't, someone else will.

— *Harvey Mackay*

Start with a smile
Most speakers don't need an introduction, just a conclusion.

— *Anonymous*

Focus on what's important
Love is patient, love is kind. It does not envy, it does not boast, it is not proud. It is not rude, it is not self-seeking, it is not easily angered, it keeps no record of wrongs. Love does not delight in evil but rejoices with the truth. It always protects, always trusts, always hopes, always perseveres. Love never fails.

— *1 Corinthians 4-8*

Break the barriers
You weren't an accident. You weren't mass produced. You aren't an assembly-line product. You were deliberately planned, specifically gifted and lovingly positioned on the Earth by the Master Craftsman.

— *Max Lucado*

Seize the summits
Remind yourself, in the darkest moments, that every failure is only a step toward success.

— *Og Mandino*

Start with a smile
You know the only people who are always sure about the proper way to raise children? Those who've never had any.

— *Bill Cosby*

Focus on what's important
If you want to know whether you are going to be a success or a failure in life, you can easily find out. The test is simple and infallible. Are you able to save money?

— *James Hill*

Break the barriers
Don't tell me something is impossible. I founded this company with a potato.

— *Herman Lay, founder of Frito-Lay*

Seize the summits
There's no thrill in easy sailing, when the skies are clear and blue.
    There's no joy in only doing things, which anyone can do.
    But there is some satisfaction that is mighty sweet to take.
    When you reach a destination that you thought you'd never make.

— *Spirella*

Start with a smile

A bird in the hand can be messy.

— Anonymous

Focus on what's important

The friend in my adversity I shall always cherish most. I can better trust those who helped to relieve the gloom of my dark hours than those who are so ready to enjoy with me the sunshine of my prosperity.

— Ulysses S. Grant

Break the barriers

When I stand before God at the end of my life, I would hope that I would not have a single bit of talent left and could say, "I used everything you gave me."

— Erma Bombeck

Seize the summits

One thing that has helped me enormously over the years is the habit of getting up early in the morning and spending the first 30 to 60 minutes reading something uplifting.

— Andrew Wood and Brian Tracy

Start with a smile
Did you hear that the communists now have a million-dollar lottery for their people? The winners get a dollar a year for a million years.

— *Ronald Reagan*

Focus on what's important
The real heroes are men and women who are friends of the poorest of the poor.

— *Nelson Mandela*

Break the barriers
Never ever ever go to see the boss about a problem without bringing along a proposed solution. Better yet, three solutions.

— *Walter Kiechel III*

Seize the summits
I work out 50 weeks a year because I want to keep getting better.

— *Derek Jeter*

Start with a smile

The best way to remember your wife's birthday is to forget it once.
— *E. Joseph Cossman*

Focus on what's important

Decide to make the evening meal an occasion – that is, begin with the understanding that when everyone is seated no disturbances will be allowed to intrude. If the ringing of an unanswered phone bothers you, turn the ringer off. If you are accustomed to watching the news, tape it and watch it later in the evening.

— *Virginia Lang and Louise Nayer*

Break the barriers

To be conscious that you are ignorant is a great step to knowledge.
— *Benjamin Disraeli*

Seize the summits

Once you have written your plan, read it aloud to yourself at least once every day. This fuels your obsession and reinforces its nature in your mind.

— *Napoleon Hill*

❧ July 24

Start with a smile

I didn't mind getting the card. The thing that bothered me was that the post office knew exactly where to deliver it.

> — *Duffy Daugherty, on receiving a letter addressed to*
> *"Duffy the Dope"*

Focus on what's important

Men turn this way and that in their search for new sources of comfort and inspiration, but the enduring truths are to be found in the Word of God.

> — *Elizabeth, the Queen Mother*

Break the barriers

We live in a time of such rapid change and growth of knowledge that only a person who continues to learn and inquire can hope to keep pace.

> — *Nathan Pusey*

Seize the summits

The opposite of quitting isn't "waiting around." No, the opposite of quitting is an invigorated new strategy designed to break the problem apart.

> — *Seth Godin*

Breakthrough Power

Start with a smile

Confidence: That quiet assured feeling you have before you fall flat on your face.

— L. Binder

Focus on what's important

Always have something beautiful in sight, even if it's just a daisy in a jelly glass.

— H. Jackson Brown, Jr.

Break the barriers

Give yourself an even greater challenge than the one you are trying to master and you will develop the powers necessary to overcome the original difficulty.

— William Bennett

Seize the summits

Many of us go through life with the brakes on. The brakes of fear, the brakes of procrastination, the brakes of unworthiness, the brakes of negative thinking. These prevent us from giving all that we have to give and sharing all that we have to share. You cannot live as though you have a thousand years to accomplish your goals. You are here today, but you may be gone tomorrow.

— Les Brown

Start with a smile

As the light changed from red to green to amber and back to red again, I sat there thinking about life. Was it nothing more than a lot of honking and yelling? Sometimes it seemed that way.

— *Jack Handey*

Focus on what's important

For a truth to be heard, it must be spoken with kindness.

— *Leo Tolstoy*

Break the barriers

You can't put your hand in a pot of glue without some of it sticking. So, too, you can't put your mind and heart into the works of the masters without some of it sticking. If you read about immortals, you increase the possibility of leaving an immortal effect. The result has been enormous for me.

— *Dr. John Demartini*

Seize the summits

It's not that I'm so smart, it's just that I stay with problems longer.

— *Albert Einstein*

Start with a smile

"Oh to be old again," said a young corpse.

— Stanislaw Lec

Focus on what's important

God Almighty first planted a garden. And indeed it is the purest of human pleasures.

— Sir Francis Bacon

Break the barriers

There's no such thing as a dead-end job. No matter what sort of work you do, your effort will make that job worthwhile.

— Russell Simmons

Seize the summits

I believe if a man sets an attainable goal for himself and works to attain it, conscious that when he does so he will then set another goal for himself, he will have a full, busy and – for this reason – a happy life.

— Lionel Barrymore

Start with a smile

The amount of time it takes for you to leave the house in the morning is directly proportional to the number of shoes in your closet.

— *Leigh Anne Jasheway*

Focus on what's important

A kind word, sincerely stated, can work magic, most notably in relationships where the magic is gone. We are never so sophisticated or so comfortable in a relationship that the little niceties can be neglected. If they are good enough for total strangers, they are certainly good enough for the people we love.

— *Leo Buscaglia*

Break the barriers

Because God knows and understands all things, He can be trusted to do what is best.

— *Billy Graham*

Seize the summits

Did I win? Did I lose? Those are the wrong questions. The correct question is: Did I make my best effort? That's what matters. The rest of it just gets in the way.

— *John Wooden*

Start with a smile
Overdrawn? But I still have checks left.

— *Anonymous*

Focus on what's important
Look around at the azaleas making fuchsia star bursts in spring; look at a full moon hanging silver on a black sky on a cold night. And realize that life is glorious, and that you have no business taking it for granted.

— *Anna Quindlen*

Break the barriers
Criticism is futile because it puts a person on the defensive and usually makes him strive to justify himself. Criticism is dangerous, because it wounds a person's precious pride, hurts his sense of importance and arouses resentment.

— *Dale Carnegie*

Seize the summits
As you set your long-range goals, let me urge you not to attempt to overcome all the obstacles before you start. Nobody would ever attempt anything of significance if all obstacles had to be removed before they started.

— *Zig Ziglar*

Start with a smile

Don't worry about avoiding temptation – as you grow older, it starts avoiding you.

— *Anonymous*

Focus on what's important

The basic thing which contributes to charm is the ability to forget oneself and be engrossed in other people.

— *Eleanor Roosevelt*

Break the barriers

It is the youngest age I have left.

— *Cato, in response to friends who questioned his decision to begin studying Greek at the age of 80*

Seize the summits

No disappointment, setback, trauma or tragedy becomes so devastating that you cannot glean something of value to take with you to the next experience. Successful people learn from everything that happens to them. They become victorious in situations where others see themselves only as victims.

— *Cherie Carter-Scott*

—

Start with a smile
The red light is always longer than the green light.
> — *Laurence Peter, Peter's Theory of Relativity*

Focus on what's important
I find that if I remind myself frequently that the purpose of life isn't to get it all done but to enjoy each step along the way and live a life filled with love, it's far easier for me to control my obsession with completing my list of things to do.
> — *Richard Carlson*

Break the barriers
Nobody makes a greater mistake than he who does nothing because he could only do a little.
> — *Edmund Burke*

Seize the summits
The quality of a man's life is in direct proportion to his commitment to excellence, regardless of his chosen field of endeavor.
> — *Vince Lombardi*

Start with a smile
I always wanted to be somebody, but I should have been more specific.

— Lily Tomlin

Focus on what's important
There's nothing that speaks of success more than the peaceful, easy confidence that one exhibits when they are living debt free.

— Wes Beavis

Break the barriers
Skill to do comes of doing.

— Ralph Waldo Emerson

Seize the summits
All we need to do to build self-confidence is select a relatively easy goal and then go ahead and accomplish it. Every time you complete a task or goal successfully, celebrate and congratulate yourself. Then set a higher goal or a more difficult task. It's just like working out with weights or running. You build up the amount of weight slowly or run farther as you develop your strength. Before long, you'll be doing things you never thought you could.

— Major William Cohen

Start with a smile
When a man with money meets a man with experience, the man with experience ends up with the money and the man with the money ends up with the experience.

— *Anonymous*

Focus on what's important
Dogs are our link to paradise. They don't know evil or jealousy or discontent. To sit with a dog on a hillside on a glorious afternoon is to be back in Eden, where doing nothing was not boring – it was peace.

— *Milan Kundera*

Break the barriers
To lengthen your life, shorten your meals.

— *Benjamin Franklin*

Seize the summits
For most of us, it's not that we don't have the ability to be great, it's that we don't devote the time. You have to put in the effort and put up with all the frustrations and obstacles.

— *Dean Simonton*

Start with a smile
I can remember way back when a liberal was someone who was generous with his own money.

— *Will Rogers*

Focus on what's important
I made a commitment to completely cut out drinking and anything that might hamper me from getting my mind and body together. And the floodgates of goodness have opened upon me – spiritually and financially.

— *Denzel Washington*

Break the barriers
We should welcome awkwardness when we're creating a new habit; it's the sign our brain is creating a pathway that will eventually make us proficient.

— *M.J. Ryan*

Seize the summits
Courage grows by daring, fear by holding back.

— *Publilius Syrus*

Start with a smile
Good judgment is the result of experience, and experience is the result of bad judgment.

— *Walter Wriston*

Focus on what's important
When you hold resentment toward another, you are bound to that person or condition by an emotional link that is stronger than steel. Forgiveness is the only way to dissolve that link and get free.

— *Catherine Ponder*

Break the barriers
One strong point is worth ten weak ones.

— *Jewish proverb*

Seize the summits
If we are involved in doing what we were put on earth to do, a joyful heart is almost guaranteed – even in the midst of deepest difficulties. Consistent and durable joy is generated when we pursue a passion that is strong enough to carry us past pain, something so meaningful and absorbing that we can ignore unhappy circumstances.

— *Thomas Kinkade*

Start with a smile

The insurance salesman said to me, "Don't let me frighten you into a hasty decision. Sleep on it tonight. If you wake up tomorrow, let me know."

— *Anonymous*

Focus on what's important

It is more noble to give yourself completely to one individual than to labor diligently for the salvation of the masses.

— *Dag Hammarskjöld*

Break the barriers

You do not have within yourself all the pieces to your puzzle. Everyone carries with them at least one and probably many pieces to someone else's puzzle. And when you present your piece, which is worthless to you, to another, you are a messenger from the Most High.

— *Rabbi Lawrence Kushner*

Seize the summits

Along any journey to success are found many enticing distractions. Discipline is the principle that defeats temptation.

— *Stephen Covey*

Start with a smile

The remaining Beatles will release yet another new song using previously recorded vocals by John Lennon. The song will be called "We're Not Home Right Now, Leave a Message After the Beep."

—Colin Quinn

Focus on what's important

Love is the long-sought Fountain of Youth. As long as we love, we remain young.

— Leo Buscaglia

Break the barriers

Real difficulties can be overcome, it is only the imaginary ones that are unconquerable.

— Theodore Vail

Seize the summits

Highly successful people are able to say no.

— Susan Collins

Start with a smile

There's no easy way to break off any relationship. It's like the mozzarella cheese on a good slice of pizza. No matter how far you pull the slice away from your mouth it just gets thinner and longer but never snaps.

— Jerry Seinfeld

Focus on what's important

When you make someone laugh, you're giving him medicine.

— Danny Kaye

Break the barriers

We go farther faster when we go together.

— Martin Luther King, Jr.

Seize the summits

Always listen to experts. They'll tell you what can't be done and why. Then do it.

— Robert Heinlein

Start with a smile

I've been on a calendar, but never on time.

— *Marilyn Monroe*

Focus on what's important

To listen to gossip both creates and encourages gossip. No listeners, no gossip.

— *A.P. Gouthey*

Break the barriers

Wise sayings are lamps that light our way, from darkness to the light of day.

— *Henry Ward Beecher*

Seize the summits

The urge to quit is the signal that an opportunity to excel is at hand.

— *Greg Quinn*

Start with a smile

Love is blind – marriage is the eye-opener.

— *Pauline Thomason*

Focus on what's important

A good reputation is more valuable than money.

— *Publilius Syrus*

Break the barriers

Obstacles cannot crush me. Every obstacle yields to stern resolve. He who is fixed to a star does not change his mind.

— *Leonardo da Vinci*

Seize the summits

Don't spend a $1.00's worth of time on a 10¢ decision.

— *Anonymous*

Start with a smile

"Aria" is Italian for "a song that will not end in your lifetime".

— *Dave Barry*

Focus on what's important

Whenever you step out of a certain comfort zone to enhance the person you wish to be, make sure you have a sense of contentment with each and every step you take. If you're doing all that you can without a sense of joy or even satisfaction, there's a strong chance you may not get to where you want to go.

— *Dave Pelzer*

Break the barriers

I never knew a man escape failures in either mind or body, who worked seven days a week.

— *Sir Robert Peel*

Seize the summits

Most people don't aim too high and miss, they aim too low and hit.

— *Bob Moawad*

Start with a smile

Advice is what we ask for when we already know the answer but wish we didn't.

— *Erica Jong*

Focus on what's important

Marriage is not a reform school.

— *Ann Landers*

Break the barriers

Demosthenes overcame his inarticulate and stammering pronunciation by speaking with pebbles in his mouth; his voice he disciplined by reciting speeches or verses when he was out of breath, while running or going up steep places.

— *Plutarch*

Seize the summits

Failure is part of learning. Fear of failure can paralyze you. If you don't risk looking ridiculous or inept or even stupid sometimes, you may stay secure, but you'll also stay the same. By avoiding failure, you're also avoiding life's richness.

— *Maria Shriver*

Start with a smile
When you have the facts on your side, argue the facts. When you have the law on your side, argue the law. When you have neither, holler.

— Al Gore

Focus on what's important
Let love and faithfulness never leave you; bind them around your neck, write them on the tablet of your heart. Then you will win favor and a good name in the sight of God and man.

— Proverbs 3:3-4

Break the barriers
We must learn never to underestimate the capacity of the human mind and body to regenerate – even when the prospects seem most wretched. What the patient expects to happen can be as potent in touching off biochemical processes as any medication.

— Norman Cousins

Seize the summits
Never answer a critic unless he's right.

— Bernard Baruch

Start with a smile

Swap: A trade between two people who think they skinned each other.

— Anonymous

Focus on what's important

There is no dignity quite so impressive, and no independence quite so important as living within your means.

— Calvin Coolidge

Break the barriers

If we think of ourselves as a raw diamond, we may curse the work of the cutter, grinder and polisher and may even call them "evil." But without their efforts, our radiant beauty would never be revealed.

— Hans Wilhelm

Seize the summits

Whenever you set out to improve your skills, change your behavior or better your family life or business, beginning in small, manageable steps gives you a greater chance of long-term success. When you start with small, achievable steps you can easily master, it reinforces your belief that you can easily improve.

— Jack Canfield

Start with a smile
We probably wouldn't worry about what people think of us if we could know how seldom they do.

— *Olin Miller*

Focus on what's important
No matter how just your words may be, you ruin everything when you speak with anger.

— *St. John Chrysostom*

Break the barriers
Men acquire a particular quality by constantly acting a particular way. We become just by performing just actions, temperate by performing temperate actions, brave by performing brave actions.

— *Aristotle*

Seize the summits
There are hazards in everything one does; but there are greater hazards in doing nothing.

— *Shirley Williams*

Start with a smile

The diamond is the hardest stone . . . to get.

— *Anonymous*

Focus on what's important

The essence of lying is in deception, not in words; a lie may be told by silence, by the accent on a syllable, by a glance of the eyes attaching a peculiar significance to a sentence; and all these kinds of lies are worse and baser by many degrees than a lie plainly worded.

— *John Ruskin*

Break the barriers

Self-pity is our worst enemy and if we yield to it, we can never do anything wise in the world.

— *Helen Keller*

Seize the summits

Undertake something that is difficult; it will do you good. Unless you try to do something beyond what you have already mastered, you will never grow.

— *Ronald Osborn*

Start with a smile

Question: How many men does it take to change a roll of toilet paper?

Answer: Nobody knows, it's never been done.

— *Anonymous*

Focus on what's important

Every calling is great when greatly pursued.

— *Oliver Wendell Holmes, Jr.*

Break the barriers

We lift ourselves by our own thoughts; we climb upon our vision of ourselves.

— *Orison Marden*

Seize the summits

Knowing what you want, doing what you love, making a difference, taking care of yourself, and continuing to grow all add meaning to life. If you find yourself wondering, "Is this all there is?" it's probably time to revisit your preferences, fine-tune your priorities and make more choices that feel right from the inside out.

— *Dr. Suzanne Zoglio*

Start with a smile
A study shows men are hit by lightning four times as often as women. Usually after saying, "I'll call you."

— Jay Leno

Focus on what's important
Happiness is produced not so much by great pieces of good fortune that seldom happen as by little advantages that occur every day.

— Benjamin Franklin

Break the barriers
In every adversity there is a seed to an equal or greater benefit.

— Brig Hart

Seize the summits
The difference in men does not lie in the size of their hands, nor in the perfection of their bodies, but in this one sublime ability of concentration: to throw the weight with the blow, to live an eternity in an hour.

— Elbert Hubbard

Start with a smile
My car has this feature that I guess is standard, because it was on my last car too. It has a rotating gas tank. Whatever side of the pump I pull up to, it's on the other side.

— *Rita Rudner*

Focus on what's important
Stay open-minded, treat your attackers fairly, listen to what they say and give them your attention whenever it is appropriate. You may learn something. Furthermore, if you do not treat them as your enemies, you make it easier for them to someday become your allies and friends.

— *Kent Keith*

Break the barriers
Read the best books, and they will improve your writing style.
— *Louisa May Alcott*

Seize the summits
A goal is a dream with a deadline.

— *Harvey Mackay*

Start with a smile

The nice thing about living in a small town like we do is that when you don't know what you're doing, someone else does.

— *Tom and Marilyn Ross*

Focus on what's important

As the purse is emptied the heart is filled.

— *Victor Hugo*

Break the barriers

Great minds discuss ideas, average minds discuss events, small minds discuss people.

— *Hugh Cameron*

Seize the summits

Calm people get trusted. Calm people get relied on. Calm people get looked up to and are given responsibility. Calm people last longer.

— *Richard Templar*

Start with a smile
Marriage is the alliance of two people, one of whom never remembers birthdays and the other who never forgets.

— *Ogden Nash*

Focus on what's important
Do something just for fun. Pleasure is one of life's essential nutrients.

— *Cheryl Richardson*

Break the barriers
It is the surmounting of difficulties that makes heroes.

— *Louis Kossuth*

Seize the summits
Do you want to know what I most regret about my youth? That I didn't dream more boldly and demand of myself more impossible things; for all one does in maturity is to carve in granite the soap bubble one blew in youth. Oh to have dreamed harder.

— *Lewis Mumford*

Start with a smile
Never play leapfrog with a unicorn.

— Anonymous

Focus on what's important
A man that studies revenge keeps his wounds green, which otherwise would heal and do well.

— Sir Francis Bacon

Break the barriers
Watching and listening – those are extremely important abilities to develop in yourself. Why, even when I was teaching, there were plenty of times when my students came up with better ideas than I had. And why shouldn't they? Just because I was the teacher didn't mean that I knew everything. No one can know it all.

— Sarah Delany

Seize the summits
There is nothing more contagious than exuberance and enthusiasm, and it is sure to get an audience.

— Harry Houdini

Start with a smile
Don't get annoyed if your neighbor plays his hi-fi at two o'clock in the morning. Call him at four and tell him how much you enjoyed it.

— *Anonymous*

Focus on what's important
Keep a grateful journal. Every night, list five things that you are grateful for. It will change your perspective of your day and your life.

— *Oprah Winfrey*

Break the barriers
A man can be short and dumpy and getting bald but if he has fire, women will like him.

— *Mae West*

Seize the summits
If you have patience, you continue doing things properly every day and sooner or later, success comes.

— *Dr. Bob Rotella*

Start with a smile

Expenditures rise to meet income.

— *Cyril Parkinson*

Focus on what's important

Make allowances for your friends' imperfections as readily as you do for your own.

— *H. Jackson Brown, Jr.*

Break the barriers

When our minds race so rapidly that we don't know which way is up, it often helps to get physical. It may seem ironic, but it works. As you focus your energy on a physical task, the traffic in your mind will begin to thin out.

— *Dr. Suzanne Zoglio*

Seize the summits

People who are consistent winners manage their challenges in hierarchical fashion. They set priorities and they live those priorities. They commit to managing their time in such a way that they do not spend time grinding along on priority number two or three or four if priority number one needs their attention.

— *Phillip McGraw*

Start with a smile

When the waitress puts the dinner on the table, the old men look at the dinner. The young men look at the waitress.

— *Gelett Burgess*

Focus on what's important

The greatest gift you can give another is the purity of your attention.

— *Dr. Richard Moss*

Break the barriers

The important thing is this: to be able at any moment to sacrifice what we are for what we could become.

— *Charles Du Boss*

Seize the summits

The mistake many people make is setting their expectations too low. Then they fail to mobilize all their talents and resources – which, in turn, lowers their self-regard and level of achievement. Resilient people access their full potential by setting clear goals that will expand their expectations.

— *Roger Crawford*

Start with a smile

We bestow on others praise in which we do not believe, on condition that in return they bestow upon us praise in which we do.

— *Jean Rostand*

Focus on what's important

Success feels sweetest when it is experienced as a fulfilled and calm spirit, free of the need to compare ourselves with what we see as the happiness and success of others.

— *Dr. Paul Pearsall*

Break the barriers

Victory is achieved before, not just during, the battle.

— *Sun Tzu*

Seize the summits

It's the action, not the fruit of the action, that's important. You have to do the right thing. It may not be in your power, may not be in your time, that there'll be any fruit. But that doesn't mean you stop doing the right thing. You may never know what results come from your action. But if you do nothing, there will be no result.

— *Mahatma Gandhi*

Start with a smile

A compromise is an arrangement whereby someone who can't get exactly what he wants makes sure nobody else gets exactly what they want.

— *Barbara Graham*

Focus on what's important

Don't think that there's going to be gold at the end of the road. Instead, value the process and you'll see that the road has been paved with gold all along.

— *Russell Simmons*

Break the barriers

To welcome a problem without resentment is to cut its size in half.

— *William Ward*

Seize the summits

If I just work when the spirit moves me, the spirit will ignore me.

— *Carolyn Forche*

Start with a smile

Everything you do irritates me. And when you're not here, the things I know you're gonna do when you come back in irritate me.

— Neil Simon

Focus on what's important

Stretch a hand to one unfriended
> And your loneliness is ended.

— John Oxenham

Break the barriers

The wisest mind has something yet to learn.

— George Santayana

Seize the summits

Don't let the sensation of fear convince you that you're too weak to have courage. Fear is the opportunity for courage, not proof of cowardice.

— John McCain

Start with a smile

The two biggest liars in the world: the guest who keeps saying, "I must be going" and the host who asks, "What's your hurry?"

— *Anonymous*

Focus on what's important

Do nothing out of selfish ambition or vain conceit, but in humility consider others better than yourselves.

— *Philippians 2:3*

Break the barriers

The best years of your life are the ones in which you decide your problems are your own. You do not blame them on your mother, the ecology or the president. You realize that you control your own destiny.

— *Albert Ellis*

Seize the summits

Goals make work more fun.

— *Joe Griffith*

Start with a smile

I know what men want. Men want to be really, really close to someone who will leave them alone.

— *Elayne Boosler*

Focus on what's important

Going to a junkyard is a sobering experience. There you can see the ultimate destination of almost everything we desire.

— *Roger von Oech*

Break the barriers

If you don't already walk and sit as if you were brought up with the Bolshoi Ballet, work on your posture. The idea is to look as if you own the world, not as if you're carrying it on your shoulders.

— *Elin Schoen*

Seize the summits

What this power is I cannot say, all I know is that it exists and it becomes available only when a man is in that state of mind in which he knows exactly what he wants and is fully determined not to quit until he finds it.

— *Alexander Graham Bell*

Start with a smile

When a man sits with a pretty girl for an hour, it seems like a minute. But let him sit on a hot stove for a minute, and it's longer than any hour. That's relativity.

— *Albert Einstein*

Focus on what's important

He who seeks the truth must listen to his opponent.

— *Isaac Reggio*

Break the barriers

Only people who have joyfully accepted themselves can take all the risks and responsibilities of being themselves.

— *Sir John Powell*

Seize the summits

Many people see discipline as the absence of freedom, when in fact it is the source of freedom.

— *Stephen Covey*

Start with a smile
A steering committee is a group of four people trying to park a car.

— *Anonymous*

Focus on what's important
Always be a first-rate version of yourself instead of a second-rate version of somebody else.

— *Judy Garland*

Break the barriers
There's no sense in worrying about things you can control, because if you can control them, there's no sense worrying. And there's no sense in worrying about things you can't control, because if you can't control them, there's no sense in worrying about them.

— *Mickey Rivers*

Seize the summits
Many things difficult to design prove easy to perform.

— *Samuel Johnson*

Start with a smile

If all the cars in the United States were placed end to end, it would probably be Labor Day Weekend.

— *Doug Larson*

Focus on what's important

One of the most difficult yet basic fundamentals to master is the art of enjoying each moment that you are given on this planet. It's easy to do that, of course, when the birds are singing and life is going your way. It's not so easy when you are struggling. Yet even the struggle is a gift, if you are willing to see it that way.

— *Isiah Thomas*

Break the barriers

I was the kind nobody thought could make it. I had a funny Boston accent. I couldn't pronounce my R's. I wasn't a beauty.

— *Barbara Walters*

Seize the summits

Be brave if you lose and meek if you win.

— *Harvey Penick*

Start with a smile

You never mention the dirt I track out.

— Anonymous, boy to mother

Focus on what's important

He who is not liberal with what he has, does but deceive himself when he thinks he would be liberal if he had more.

— William Plumer

Break the barriers

I love the man that can smile in trouble, that can gather strength from distress and grow brave by reflection.

— Thomas Paine

Seize the summits

The world has expanded in almost all directions, but we still have a twenty-four-hour day. The most successful people and the most unsuccessful people all receive the same ration of hours each day.

— Stanley Marcus

Start with a smile
I have an inferiority complex. But it's not a very good one.
— *Steven Wright*

Focus on what's important
Those who first accept the silence of obscurity are best qualified to handle the applause of popularity.
— *Charles Swindoll*

Break the barriers
Accomplishment is 85 percent attitude and 15 percent skill.
— *Zig Ziglar*

Seize the summits
As any change must begin somewhere, it is the single individual who will experience it and carry it through. The change must indeed begin with an individual; it might be any one of us. Nobody can afford to look around and to wait for somebody else to do what he is unwilling to do himself.
— *Carl Jung*

Start with a smile

A lot of friction is caused by half the drivers trying to go fast enough to thrill their girlfriends and the other half trying to go slow enough to placate their wives.

— *Bill Vaughan*

Focus on what's important

To have integrity, you do not lie or cheat on the small things; and, as a result, you are not corrupted by the larger temptations – the lure of power, prestige or money.

— *Adrian Gostick and Dana Telford*

Break the barriers

Man would not have attained the possible unless time and again he had reached out for the impossible.

— *Max Weber*

Seize the summits

I think we should all set goals in life and set them high. I did that, and my parents encouraged me to do it, which is one of the main reasons I am where I am today.

— *Derek Jeter*

Start with a smile

What makes certain people popular? That depends. In third grade, it's the simple ability to stuff two dimes up your nose.

— *Dennis Miller*

Focus on what's important

One does not fall "in" or "out" of love. One grows in love.

— *Leo Buscaglia*

Break the barriers

Perfection is attained by slow degrees. It requires the hand of time.

— *Voltaire*

Seize the summits

One thing I've noticed in all my years of coaching is that the most successful athletes, the most successful people in all walks of life, in fact, have one thing in common – they persist. They refuse to let anyone tell them their dreams can't come true. They never waver in their belief in themselves. They refuse to be denied.

— *Rick Pitino*

Start with a smile
Women don't want to hear what you think. Women want to hear what they think, in a deeper voice.

— *Bill Cosby*

Focus on what's important
The basic remedy for most couples is for each to give more to the other.

— *Dr. Theodore Rubin*

Break the barriers
When your search for a solution begins to drain your energy, it's time to tap your brain trust. We all have around us a team of geniuses – just waiting to be asked for their ideas. Coworkers, bosses, spouses, children, siblings, friends and family all have the potential of sharing exactly the idea that you need at any given moment.

— *Suzanne Zoglio*

Seize the summits
Faith is to believe what you do not see; the reward of this faith is to see what you believe.

— *St. Augustine*

Start with a smile
People are either hunting for husbands or hiding from them.
— *Oscar Wilde*

Focus on what's important
Once you free your notion of self-worth from the bonds of material things, you will need less and you will spend less. As your self-esteem rises, your debt will diminish.
— *Suze Orman*

Break the barriers
Change has a considerable psychological impact on the human mind. To the fearful it is threatening because it means that things may get worse. To the hopeful it is encouraging because things may get better. To the confident it is inspiring because the challenge exists to make things better.
— *King Whitney, Jr.*

Seize the summits
No one can arrive from being talented alone. God gives talent; work transforms talent into genius.
— *Anna Pavlova*

Start with a smile
Screens: The wire mesh that keeps flies from getting out of the house.

— Anonymous

Focus on what's important
I credit my youthfulness at 80 to the fact of a cheerful disposition and contentment in every period of my life with what I was.
— Oliver Wendell Holmes

Break the barriers
I murmured because I had no shoes, until I met a man who had no feet.

— Persian proverb

Seize the summits
Remember that the quickest way to get a raise is to raise your commitment to the company.

— H. Jackson Brown, Jr.

Start with a smile

People tell me, "Gee, you look good." There are three ages of man: youth, middle age and "Gee, you look good."

— *Red Skelton*

Focus on what's important

One of the symptoms of an approaching nervous breakdown is the belief that one's work is terribly important, and that to take a vacation would bring all kinds of disaster. If I were a medical man, I should prescribe a vacation to any patient who considered his work important.

— *Bertrand Russell*

Break the barriers

A cheerful disposition is a fund of ready capital, a magnet for the good things of life.

— *Orison Marden*

Seize the summits

Nothing is so fatiguing as the eternal hanging on of an uncompleted task.

— *William James*

Start with a smile

There's no secret about success. Did you ever know a successful man that didn't tell you all about it?

— *Kin Hubbard*

Focus on what's important

One of my favorite perks during fair weather is to simply take a book out into the sunshine. After lunch I pull up a chair on my patio and spend ten minutes or so basking and browsing. The combination of the warm sun, the absorbing words and the pure relaxation is almost guaranteed to lift my spirits and send me back to work with a higher joy-quotient.

— *Thomas Kinkade*

Break the barriers

Count your blessings every day. Make the list as long as you can. If you are fortunate enough to have it, start with health. Add the love of children and family. From there, it's easy to build the list.

— *Jeffrey Gitomer*

Seize the summits

Opportunities multiply as they are seized; they die when neglected. Life is a long line of opportunities.

— *John Wicker*

Start with a smile
Going to the opera, like getting drunk, is a sin that carries its own punishment with it.

— *Hannah More*

Focus on what's important
Get a life in which you notice the smell of salt water pushing itself on a breeze over the dunes, a life in which you stop and watch how a red-tailed hawk circles over a pond and a stand of pines. Get a life in which you pay attention to the baby as she scowls with concentration when she tries to pick up a Cheerio with her thumb and first finger.

— *Anna Quindlen*

Break the barriers
He who would not eat forbidden fruit must stay away from the forbidden tree.

— *Anonymous*

Seize the summits
Keeping promises you've made to yourself – from cleaning the garage to applying for a new job – speaks volumes about your personal integrity.

— *Dr. Suzanne Zoglio*

Start with a smile
Minor surgery is what other people have.

— *Bill Watson*

Focus on what's important
When in doubt, lean to the side of mercy.

— *Miguel de Cervantes*

Break the barriers
Find those persons in whose presence you feel more energetic, more creative and more able to pursue your life goals. Stay away from persons who make you feel apprehensive, or who influence you to doubt yourself. Especially, stay away from those persons who drain you, so that your energy is all used up trying to maintain the relationship.

— *Dennis Augustine*

Seize the summits
The size of our past goals has determined our present life style. The size of our future goals will determine our future life style.

— *Danny Cox*

Start with a smile

Writing is easy. All you do is stare at a blank sheet of paper until drops of blood form on your forehead.

— *Gene Fowler*

Focus on what's important

The probability that we may fail in the struggle ought not to deter us from the support of a cause we believe to be just.

— *Abraham Lincoln*

Break the barriers

To weep is to make less the depth of grief.

— *William Shakespeare*

Seize the summits

Don't ask what the world needs. Ask what makes you come alive, and go do it. Because what the world needs is people who have come alive.

— *Howard Thurman*

Start with a smile
The English church-goer prefers a severe preacher because he thinks a few home truths will do his neighbors no harm.

— George Bernard Shaw

Focus on what's important
He has honor if he holds himself to an ideal of conduct though it is inconvenient, unprofitable or dangerous to do so.

— Walter Lippman

Break the barriers
You will attract more people to you if you act and speak from abundance rather than scarcity.

— Brian Koslow

Seize the summits
The spirit, the will to win, and the will to excel are the things that endure. These qualities are so much more important than the events that occur.

— Vince Lombardi

Start with a smile

Insect repellent: One of the number of "gag" items available in the novelty sections of tackle shops, along with "waterproof" clothing, "damp-proof" matches and "long-life" batteries.

— *Henry Beard and Roy McKie*

Focus on what's important

People with many interests live not only longest, but happiest.

— *George Matthew Allen*

Break the barriers

I have seen what a laugh can do. It can transform almost unbearable tears into something bearable, even hopeful.

— *Bob Hope*

Seize the summits

Even if it's just for 15 minutes, pursue one of your passions every day. Watch your health and esteem grow as you feed your soul through regular exercise of passionate interest.

— *Dr. Ellen McGrath*

Start with a smile

Now we sit through Shakespeare in order to recognize the quotations.

— *Orson Welles*

Focus on what's important

No man is so poor as to have nothing worth giving: as well might the mountain streams say they have nothing to give the sea because they are not rivers. Give what you have. To someone it may be better than you dare to think.

— *Henry Wadsworth Longfellow*

Break the barriers

Courage is like a muscle; it's strengthened by use.

— *Anonymous*

Seize the summits

Effort only fully releases its reward after a person refuses to quit.

— *Napoleon Hill*

Start with a smile

I'm here to speak, and you're here to listen, and if you finish before me, feel free to leave.

— Adlai Stevenson

Focus on what's important

A successful way to determine how much we truly care for someone is to discern how high their happiness and welfare are on our priority list.

— Leo Buscaglia

Break the barriers

Wise men change their minds, fools never.

— English proverb

Seize the summits

Sometimes, the only difference between a successful person and a failure is that the successful person has the courage to get started, to do something, to begin moving toward accomplishing a specific goal.

— Andrew Wood and Brian Tracy

Start with a smile

To judge from the covers of countless women's magazines, the two topics most interesting to women are 1) why men are all disgusting pigs and 2) how to attract men.

— *Dave Barry*

Focus on what's important

Integrity is keeping my commitment even if the circumstances when I made the commitment have changed.

— *David Jeremiah*

Break the barriers

Never go to bed angry. Say what annoys you, then finish with "I love you." Trust me, it makes the morning brighter.

— *Joan Rivers*

Seize the summits

Admit when you're wrong. When I'm courageous enough to admit I'm wrong or I've made a mistake, I'm amazed at the generosity of the person on the receiving end. This increases trust, elevates credibility and strengthens the relationship.

— *Vickie Milazzo*

Start with a smile
I don't like spinach, and I'm glad I don't, because if I liked it I'd eat it, and I just hate it.

— *Clarence Darrow*

Focus on what's important
Happiness is different from pleasure. Happiness has something to do with struggling and enduring and accomplishments.

— *George Sheenan*

Break the barriers
What sculpture is to a block of marble, education is to the soul.

— *Joseph Addison*

Seize the summits
Motivation doesn't really exist outside of action. Motivation is movement. By taking action, by setting out along the path, we start the process, we create our own motivation.

— *Anthony Grant and Jane Greene*

Start with a smile
I like the way you always manage to state the obvious with a sense of real discovery.

— Gore Vidal

Focus on what's important
If I find myself a desire which no experience in this world can satisfy, the most probable explanation is that I was made for another world.

— C.S. Lewis

Break the barriers
In any man's dark hour, a pat on the back and an earnest hand-clasp may well work a small miracle.

— Brigadier General S.L.A. Marshall

Seize the summits
One half of knowing what you want is knowing what you must give up before you get it.

— Sidney Howard

Start with a smile
Nothing is more responsible for the good old days than a bad memory.

— Franklin Adams

Focus on what's important
Because I can easily get involved with my vocation and rationalize time away from my children, I reevaluate on a regular basis. I often ask my wife if she feels I am spending enough time with our children. I also ask our children the same question.

— Gary Smalley

Break the barriers
When you feel isolated, seek out someone who is alone. When you feel forsaken, comfort one who has been abandoned. When you feel impoverished, give to the poor. When you feel unloved, love a child.

— Greg Quinn

Seize the summits
The time to repair the roof is when the sun is shining.

— John F. Kennedy

Start with a smile
The girl had long black hair and wore long black gloves to cover it.
— *Anonymous*

Focus on what's important
The smile reaches down deeply and relaxes us. A doctor would not be able to find anything in his medicine bag that takes effect so quickly, so harmoniously.

— *Alain*

Break the barriers
Don't find fault. Find a remedy.

— *Henry Ford*

Seize the summits
Life is an adventure. Don't be afraid to get off the beaten path because very few have already trod there. You can go down a side way and if you've made a mistake, what does it really matter? As long as you are learning from the mistake, success will ultimately rub off on you.

— *William Shatner*

Start with a smile

Nothing reminds a woman of all that needs to be done around the house like a husband who is taking it easy.

— *Bob Phillips*

Focus on what's important

Do not keep the alabaster boxes of your love and tenderness sealed up until your friends are dead. Fill their lives with sweetness. Speak approving, cheering words while their ears can hear them and while their hearts can be thrilled by them.

— *Henry Ward Beecher*

Break the barriers

Success in business does not depend upon genius. Any young man of ordinary intelligence who is normally sound and not afraid to work should succeed in spite of obstacles and handicaps if he plays the game fairly and keeps everlastingly at it.

— *J.C. Penney*

Seize the summits

Sacrifice and self-denial lie behind every success.

— *Vince Lombardi*

Start with a smile

A man with parents alive is a fifteen-year-old boy.

— *Philip Roth*

Focus on what's important

Resistance, whether to one's appetites or to the ways of the world, is a chief factor in the shaping of character.

— *Eric Hoffer*

Break the barriers

Never be disagreeable just because you disagree.

— *John Wooden*

Seize the summits

That impossible dream you dreamed when you were young but got talked out of, the one you thought you outgrew, might be the key to awakening your genius. That special talent you never followed through on might be an important source of delight, the one you should commit to. That old dream might be the one thing that will bring the magic of meaning to your life.

— *Mark Hansen and Barbara Nichols*

Start with a smile

We are living in the kind of country where we find the average citizen is one who as soon as he is able to afford a Chevrolet buys a Cadillac.

— *Anonymous*

Focus on what's important

When we were growing up, we ate all of our meals together. Supper was the most special time, when we could talk about our day and just enjoy each other's company. It was comforting, and it was fun.

— *Elizabeth Delany*

Break the barriers

The secret of genius is to carry the spirit of the child into old age, which means never losing your enthusiasm.

— *Aldous Huxley*

Seize the summits

The greatest pleasure in life is doing what people say you cannot do.

— *Walter Bagehot*

Start with a smile
When in love try not to say foolish things; if you succeed, you are not in love.

— *Anonymous*

Focus on what's important
First find something you like to do so much you'd gladly do it for nothing; then learn to do it so well people are happy to pay you for it.

— *Walt Disney*

Break the barriers
Every small, positive change we can make in ourselves repays us in confidence in the future.

— *Alice Walker*

Seize the summits
When boredom threatens your desire to keep working on something, you have to start looking for new ways to stimulate your mind, to make sure what you're doing is fun and interesting again.

— *Rick Pitino*

Start with a smile

The person in my household who seems to know the most about parenting is my ten-year-old daughter. Of course, she seems to know the most about everything under the sun. She will, undoubtedly, get smarter and smarter until the day she gives birth to her first child.

— Karen Linamen

Focus on what's important

We forgive to the extent that we love.

— François de La Rochefoucauld

Break the barriers

Although the world is full of suffering, it is also full of the overcoming of it.

— Helen Keller

Seize the summits

If a man writes a better book, preaches a better sermon or makes a better mousetrap than his neighbor, though he build his house in the woods, the world will make a beaten path to his door.

— Ralph Waldo Emerson

Start with a smile
A pun is the lowest form of humor – if you don't think of it first.
— *Oscar Levant*

Focus on what's important
About ninety percent of the things in our lives are right and about ten percent are wrong. If we want to be happy, all we have to do is to concentrate on the ninety percent that are right and ignore the ten percent that are wrong.
— *Dale Carnegie*

Break the barriers
Comfort and prosperity have never enriched the world as much as adversity. Out of pain and problems have come the sweetest song, the most touching poems, the most gripping stories and inspiring lives.
— *Billy Graham*

Seize the summits
The rewards for those who persevere far exceed the pain that precedes the victory.
— *Karen Livingston*

Start with a smile

For every person who wants to teach there are approximately thirty who don't want to learn.

— W.C. Sellar and R.J. Yeatman

Focus on what's important

Many times a word of praise or thanks or appreciation or cheer has kept a man on his feet. Blessed is the man who speaks such a word.

— William Barclay

Break the barriers

Having a healthy, balanced life is essential for superior results. You cannot be fully engaged in your work if you are tired or worried about something else.

— Marilyn Tam

Seize the summits

You've got to commit yourself to an act or a vision that pulls you further than you want to go and forces you to use your hidden strengths.

— John Johnson

Start with a smile

You can always spot a well-informed man – his views are the same as yours.

— *Ilka Chase*

Focus on what's important

To the world, you may be just one person, but to one person you may be the world.

— *Josephine Billings*

Break the barriers

Solon, the sage of Athens, was asked the secret of strength and youth. He replied: "I learn something new every day."

— *Orison Marden*

Seize the summits

A real decision is measured by the fact that you've taken new action. If there's no action, you haven't truly decided. A critical rule I've made for myself is never to leave the scene of a decision without first taking a specific action toward its realization.

— *Anthony Robbins*

Start with a smile

Literary critic: A person who can find a meaning in literature that the author didn't know was there.

— Anonymous

Focus on what's important

Frugality makes a poor man rich.

— Seneca

Break the barriers

Exercise promotes the psychological benefits of looking and feeling healthy, and it reduces stress and stress-induced eating.

— Dr. Richard Couey

Seize the summits

Those who truly have the spirit of champions are never wholly happy with an easy win. Half the satisfaction stems from knowing it was the time and effort you invested that led to your high achievement.

— Nicole Haislett

Start with a smile

Recession is when your neighbor loses his job. Depression is when you lose yours. And recovery is when Jimmy Carter loses his.

— *Ronald Reagan*

Focus on what's important

To love is to give one's time. We never give the impression that we care when we are in a hurry.

— *Paul Tournier*

Break the barriers

Have confidence that if you have done a little thing well, you can do a bigger thing well too.

— *Joseph Storey*

Seize the summits

One can choose to go back toward safety or forward toward growth. Growth must be chosen again and again; fear must be overcome again and again.

— *Abraham Maslow*

Start with a smile
I don't have a girlfriend. But I do know a woman who'd be mad at me for saying that.

— *Mitch Hedberg*

Focus on what's important
Once we assuage our conscience by calling something a "necessary evil," it begins to look more and more necessary and less and less evil.

— *Sydney Harris*

Break the barriers
I am always doing that which I cannot do, in order that I may learn how to do it.

— *Pablo Picasso*

Seize the summits
You can't let negativity get in your ear. Your ear is like an embryo. Negative ideas will grow in there if you're not careful. There are always going to be critics trying to dull your dreams. But you can't let them.

— *Russell Simmons*

Start with a smile

You can leave the motel bed unmade.

> — *Anonymous, on why it's great to be a man*

Focus on what's important

One of the most tragic things I know about human nature is that all of us tend to put off living. We are all dreaming of some magical rose garden over the horizon – instead of enjoying the roses that are blooming outside our windows today.

> — *Dale Carnegie*

Break the barriers

Dress like today is important. If you dress for each day expectantly, importantly, fashionably, then each day will become that. People will react differently to you if you dress as if it matters – and you'll react differently to that different reaction. It's an upward spiral.

> — *Richard Templar*

Seize the summits

I thatched my roof when the sun was shining, and now I am not afraid of the storm.

> — *George Stivers*

Start with a smile
No matter how much cats fight, there always seem to be plenty of kittens.

— Abraham Lincoln

Focus on what's important
Whatever is begun in anger ends in shame.

— Benjamin Franklin

Break the barriers
A pessimist sees the difficulty in every opportunity; an optimist sees the opportunity in every difficulty.

— Sir Winston Churchill

Seize the summits
Once you have determined your definite major purpose, you will begin to budget your time and your money and all your day-to-day endeavors so that they will lead to the attainment of your major purpose. Time budgeting always pays dividends because each moment is made to progress toward your goal.

— Napoleon Hill

Start with a smile

Cricket: A game which the English, not being a spiritual people, have invented in order to give themselves some conception of eternity.

— *Stormont Mancroft*

Focus on what's important

Laughter is the brush that sweeps away the cobwebs of the heart.

— *Mort Walker*

Break the barriers

Though you are a prudent old man, do not despise counsel.

— *Spanish proverb*

Seize the summits

Prepare yourself for greater success by putting yourself totally into what you are doing now, even if it isn't your "ultimate." Fully engaging yourself in the present not only helps you to enjoy what you are doing but also prepares you mentally to handle the greater challenges and responsibilities that will come with the attainment of your goals.

— *Laurence Boldt*

Start with a smile
If you want an accurate picture of the time it will take to install something, you need to use a different formula altogether: Calculate the worst-case-scenario amount of time you would be willing to spend on this project, then multiply by four.
— *Karen Linamen*

Focus on what's important
Never esteem anything as of advantage to you that will make you break your word or lose your self-respect.
— *Marcus Aurelius Antoninus*

Break the barriers
The most handicapped person in the world is a negative thinker.
— *Heather Whitestone, Miss America 1994, who is deaf*

Seize the summits
Neither should a ship rely on one small anchor, nor should life rest on a single hope.
— *Epictetus*

❧ October 8

Start with a smile
Second story man: The fellow whose wife doesn't believe his first story.

— *Anonymous*

Focus on what's important
We were never meant to lose our playful spirit as we reach adulthood. Neither are we to divide our world rigidly into "serious" work and "relaxing" leisure. The lines are supposed to cross. We live far more joyfully when we allow ourselves a playful spirit even in our work and when we inject meaning and purpose into our play.

— *Thomas Kinkade*

Break the barriers
What lies behind us and what lies before us are tiny matters compared to what lies within us.

— *Ralph Waldo Emerson*

Seize the summits
It's not what we do once in a while that shapes our lives, but what we do consistently.

— *Anthony Robbins*

Start with a smile

By all means marry; if you get a good wife, you'll be happy. If you get a bad one, you'll become a philosopher.

— Socrates

Focus on what's important

Some people fear that when beauty fades, so does love. In reality, it is the other way around; beauty fades only when love is gone.

— Leo Buscaglia

Break the barriers

I love my enemies for two reasons: They inspire me to recognize my weakness. They also inspire me to perfect my imperfect nature.

— Sri Chinmoy

Seize the summits

When you find many people applauding you for what you do, and a few condemning, you can be certain that you are on the wrong course because you're doing the things that fools approve of. When the crowd ridicules and scorns you, you can at least know one thing, that it is at least possible that you are acting wisely.

— E.W. Scripps

Start with a smile

The only great acting we see nowadays is from the losing nominees on Oscar Night.

— *Will Rogers*

Focus on what's important

Part of achieving happiness is learning to enjoy even the less invigorating parts of the journey.

— *Stephen Covey*

Break the barriers

The more you seek security, the less of it you have. But the more you seek opportunity, the more likely it is that you will achieve the security that you desire.

— *Brian Tracy*

Seize the summits

What success I achieved in the theater is due to the fact that I have always worked just as hard when there were 10 people in the house as when there were thousands, just as hard in Springfield, Illinois, as on Broadway.

— *Bojangles Robinson*

Start with a smile
A nickel will get you on the subway, but garlic will get you a seat.
— *New York Jewish saying*

Focus on what's important
The goal in marriage is not to think alike, but to think together.
— *Robert Dodds*

Break the barriers
Life is like the wrong side of a carpet. We see many different colored threads running every which way. They seem to make no sense at all. But one day in this life or thereafter, we will see the right side of the carpet and then we will realize that everything has made a perfect pattern.
— *Hans Wilhelm*

Seize the summits
I never wrote anything that was published until I was forty.
— *James Michener*

Start with a smile
A married couple can best be defined as a unit of people whose sleep habits are carefully engineered to keep each other awake.
— *Mary Roach*

Focus on what's important
True greatness, true leadership, is achieved not by reducing men to one's service but in giving oneself in selfless service to them.
— *Oswald Sanders*

Break the barriers
When you improve a little each day, eventually big things occur.
— *John Wooden*

Seize the summits
A man should never be ashamed to admit he was wrong, which is but saying, that he is wiser today than he was yesterday.
— *Alexander Pope*

Start with a smile

Hubert, a speech, to be immortal, doesn't have to be eternal.
— *Muriel Humphrey, to her husband*

Focus on what's important

If you judge people, you have no time to love them.
— *Mother Teresa*

Break the barriers

Don't be reckless with your health. When I was young, I thought I was God Almighty. Then I had a heart attack at age 34. My doctor told me I had "Superman Syndrome." He says that when a guy feels good, he thinks he's Superman. He only goes to the doctor when the kryptonite gets him.
— *Ralph Haas*

Seize the summits

The cure for boredom is not diversion, it is to find some work to do, something to care about.
— *John Gardner*

Start with a smile
One girl to another: "I can only stand him for an hour. He gets tired of listening after that."

— Salo

Focus on what's important
It is wiser to err on the side of generosity than on the side of scrutiny.

— Max Lucado

Break the barriers
As a physician, I have seen men, after all other therapy had failed, lifted out of disease and melancholy by the serene effort of prayer.

— Alexis Carrel

Seize the summits
Only those who dare to fail greatly can ever achieve greatly.

— Herodotus

Start with a smile

You know you're going out with someone too young for you when they say, "Did you know Paul McCartney was in a band before Wings?"

— Anonymous

Focus on what's important

A man should hear a little music, read a little poetry and see a fine picture every day of his life, in order that worldly cares may not obliterate the sense of the beautiful which God has implanted in the human soul.

— Johann von Goethe

Break the barriers

Adversity is the breakfast of champions.

— Rick Godwin

Seize the summits

Your goal should be just out of reach, but not out of sight.

— Denis Waitley and Remi Witt

Start with a smile

Experience is what you get when you don't get what you want.

— *Dan Stanford*

Focus on what's important

It's just as important to listen to someone with your eyes as it is with your ears.

— *Martin Buxbaum*

Break the barriers

Within us all there are wells of thought and dynamos of energy which are not suspected until emergencies arise. Then oftentimes we find that it is comparatively simple to double or triple our former capacities and to amaze ourselves by the results achieved.

— *Thomas Watson*

Seize the summits

The most successful people make decisions rapidly because they are clear on their values and what they really want for their lives.

— *Anthony Robbins*

Start with a smile
I've learned one thing – people who know the least seem to know it the loudest.

— Andy Capp

Focus on what's important
Until you make peace with who you are, you'll never be content with what you have.

— Doris Mortman

Break the barriers
If you're not learning while you're earning, you're cheating yourself out of the better portion of your compensation.

— Napoleon Hill

Seize the summits
Working a high-pressure job for a difficult boss is a challenge. You're going to get upset, but how you handle getting upset will speak volumes about your ability to stay above it and succeed.

— Yogi Berra

Start with a smile
Perfume: Any smell that is used to drown a worse one.
— *Elbert Hubbard*

Focus on what's important
Only two days separate those who are living in prosperity and those who are not – yesterday and tomorrow. Prosperous people live on yesterday's money. Impoverished people live on tomorrow's money. Yesterday's money is your savings. Tomorrow's money is money you haven't got, so you borrow it from someone else.
— *Wes Beavis*

Break the barriers
Adversity is the state in which a man most easily becomes acquainted with himself, being free from flatterers.
— *Samuel Johnson*

Seize the summits
All acts performed in the world begin in the imagination.
— *Barbara Harrison*

Start with a smile
Antique: An object which has made a round trip to the attic.
— *Anonymous*

Focus on what's important
Spending time with a child is an open window to peace and happiness. When we are in the presence of a newborn, we have a powerful reminder of the magnificent mystery and magic of life.
— *Susyn Reeve*

Break the barriers
Friends, relatives, peers, classmates; they were all dying. I had no indication of any trouble, but I began to get a fear of developing heart disease. I knew there was a better way to live, and I knew it was about time I did something about it.
— *Dr. Paul Spangler, on why he started running at age 69 and why he ran the New York City marathon at age 92*

Seize the summits
The enemy is in front of us, behind us, to the left of us and to the right of us. They can't escape us this time!
— *Lewis Puller, marine lieutenant*

❧ October 20

Start with a smile
Book: Handy package containing varying amounts of low-grade toilet paper for emergency use on long hikes through the deep woods, at remote campsites or in poorly equipped lodges.

— Henry Beard and Roy McKie

Focus on what's important
The higher we are placed, the more humble we should walk.

— Cicero

Break the barriers
Most of the things worth doing in the world had been declared impossible before they were done.

— Louis Brandeis

Seize the summits
Self-respect is the fruit of discipline: the sense of dignity grows with the ability to say no to oneself.

— Abraham Heschel

Start with a smile

Futon is a Japanese word that means "sore back."

— *Nick Arnette*

Focus on what's important

Love your home – its physical space, its personal history, the relationships that define it. Cherishing a home means first of all that you speak well of it. You look for its good points and share those with outsiders; you avoid holding up its faults to the glare of outside opinion.

— *Thomas Kinkade*

Break the barriers

The most disturbing and wasteful emotions in modern life, next to fright, are those which are associated with the idea of blame, directed against the self or against others.

— *Marilyn Ferguson*

Seize the summits

Everybody is looking for instant success, but it doesn't work that way. You build a successful life one day at a time.

— *Lou Holtz*

Start with a smile
Tell a man that there are 500 billion stars in the universe and he will believe you. Tell him a fence has just been painted and he has to touch it to find out that it has been.

— Herb Cohen

Focus on what's important
Try to be happy in this very present moment; don't wait for a better day.

— Thomas Fuller

Break the barriers
Much of your life can be healthy and satisfying, but if an important part of it is not working well, you will not feel fulfilled. Successful living is not a matter of success in the workplace or success at home; it is the product of their combination.

— Dr. David Niven

Seize the summits
I wanted to be scared again. I wanted to feel unsure again. That's the only way I learn, the only way I feel challenged.

— Connie Chung

Start with a smile
Rare volume: A returned book.

— *Harry Herschelovitzer*

Focus on what's important
A man who reforms himself has contributed his full share towards the reformation of his neighbor.

— *Norman Douglas*

Break the barriers
Try to do what you already know; and in doing so, you will in good time discover the hidden things you now inquire about.

— *Rembrandt*

Seize the summits
You must have a purpose for each day. This gives each day a structure and the sense you are controlling the day and not being controlled by it. Purpose establishes your discipline and makes you more focused.

— *Rick Pitino*

Start with a smile
A high school in Connecticut has a power-nap club. We called that algebra class.

— *Jay Leno*

Focus on what's important
I consider the most enviable of titles the character of an honest man.

— *George Washington*

Break the barriers
Reflect upon your present blessings, of which every man has many; not on your past misfortunes, of which all men have some.

— *Charles Dickens*

Seize the summits
When I talked, no one listened to me. But as soon as I acted I became persuasive, and I no longer find anyone skeptical.

— *Gkosue Borsi*

Start with a smile

I was introduced to a beautiful young lady as a man in his nineties. Early nineties, I insisted.

— *George Burns*

Focus on what's important

The habit of saving is itself an education; it fosters every virtue, teaches self-denial, cultivates the sense of order, trains to think ahead and so broadens the mind.

— *Theodore Munger*

Break the barriers

Faith is not believing that God can, but that God will.

— *Abraham Lincoln*

Seize the summits

The man who makes no mistakes lacks boldness and the spirit of adventure. He never tries anything new. He is a brake on the wheels of progress.

— *M.W. Lamour*

Start with a smile
As anyone who has ever tried to purchase a PC knows, computer technology moves fast. No matter which computer you buy, no matter how much you spend, by the time you get it to your car – it's an eight-track tape player.
— *Dennis Miller*

Focus on what's important
He who covers over an offense promotes love, but whoever repeats the matter separates close friends.
— *Proverbs 17:9*

Break the barriers
When you have shut the doors, and darkened your room, remember never to say that you are alone; for God is within.
— *Epictetus*

Seize the summits
Genius is nothing but a great aptitude for patience.
— *Benjamin Franklin*

Start with a smile
When you're rich, people say you're profound, handsome, grace-ful – and sing like an angel.

— Jewish proverb

Focus on what's important
Friendship makes prosperity more brilliant, and lightens adver-sity by dividing and sharing it.

— Cicero

Break the barriers
A short saying often contains much wisdom.

— Sophocles

Seize the summits
The great man is the man who does a thing for the first time.

— Alexander Smith

Start with a smile

Monopolist: A man who keeps an elbow on each arm of the theater chair.

— *Anonymous*

Focus on what's important

The greatest use of life is to spend it for something that will outlast it.

— *William James*

Break the barriers

When we are in the company of sensible people, we ought to be doubly cautious of talking too much, lest we lose two good things, their good opinion and our own improvement; for what we have to say we know, but what they have to say we know not.

— *Charles Caleb Colton*

Seize the summits

Focus on the wildly important. People are naturally wired to focus on only one thing at a time (or at best, very few) with excellence.

— *Stephen Covey*

Start with a smile
Men who have a pierced ear are better prepared for marriage – they've experienced pain and bought jewelry.

— *Rita Rudner*

Focus on what's important
The best antidote I know for comparison compulsion (or status-symbol syndrome, as it's also known) is service. Not serving just anyone, but serving people who can't give you anything of value in return.

— *Kerry and Chris Shook*

Break the barriers
Books are the compasses and telescopes and sextants and charts which other men have prepared to help us navigate the dangerous seas of human life.

— *Jesse Bennett*

Seize the summits
Setting an example is not the main means of influencing others, it is the only means.

— *Albert Einstein*

Start with a smile

I was working on the proof of one of my poems all morning, and took out a comma. In the afternoon I put it back again.

— *Oscar Wilde*

Focus on what's important

If I had a party to attend and didn't want to be there, I would play the part of someone who was having a lovely time.

— *Shirley MacLaine*

Break the barriers

The next time you find yourself in an argument, rather than defend your position, see if you can see the other point of view first.

— *Richard Carlson*

Seize the summits

When I'm low on energy, exercise recharges me. It also relieves stress. A vigorous workout restores perspective and helps me release concerns that had seemed deserving of worry.

— *Tom Gegax*

Start with a smile

Deep down inside, men are biological creatures, like jellyfish or trees, only less likely to clean the bathroom.

— *Dave Barry*

Focus on what's important

If you want people to notice your faults, start giving advice.

— *Kelly Stephens*

Break the barriers

Conditions are never just right. People who delay action until all factors are favorable do nothing.

— *William Feather*

Seize the summits

No person has done anything great without first dreaming great dreams. Let your mind go. Think outside the lines. And don't let anyone tell you to think small. Go in a new direction. After all, you'll never succeed beyond your wildest dreams – unless you have some pretty wild dreams.

— *John Maxwell*

Start with a smile

No one appreciates the very special genius of your conversation as a dog does. If you chat with him a while, gradually building up the argument and the intonation, he relishes it so that he will roll all around the floor, lie on his back kicking and groaning with joyous worship. Very few wives are so affected.

— Christopher Morley

Focus on what's important

Forgiveness without forgetting is not forgiveness at all – only an empty gesture. Forgiveness is the real thing only when we struggle and succeed in putting the hurt behind us. This makes us truly free of it so that it does not impede our love – much as a pebble in a shoe hurts the foot with each step taken.

— Dr. Theodore Rubin

Break the barriers

No man can tell another his faults so as to benefit him, unless he loves him.

— Henry Ward Beecher

Seize the summits

Not to decide is to decide.

— Harvey Cox

Start with a smile
I wasn't kissing her, I was whispering in her mouth.

— *Chico Marx*

Focus on what's important
I was never more unhappy than when I had won five Gold Medals. It's kind of ironic, isn't it?

— *Matt Biondi*

Break the barriers
If experience was so important, we'd never have had anyone walk on the moon.

— *Doug Rader*

Seize the summits
In 1974, I blacksmithed the now famous clunker from scavenged objects. Then I started to hear that high form of recognition: "You can't do that," and "It won't work." I knew I was onto something big.

— *Gary Fisher, mountain bike designer*

Start with a smile
I was humble for a few weeks, but nobody noticed.
— *Katherine Whitehorn*

Focus on what's important
Do not spoil what you have by desiring what you don't have;
remember that what you now have was once among the things
only hoped for.
— *Epicurus*

Break the barriers
There are many things you can learn from someone who is close
to you. That's why I don't think your role models have to be
famous people. Your best role models can be the people you
see and talk to every day.
— *Derek Jeter*

Seize the summits
All successful employers are stalking men who will do the
unusual, men who think, men who attract attention by performing more than is expected of them.
— *Charles Schwab*

Start with a smile
Smoking is one of the leading causes of statistics.
— *Fletcher Knebel*

Focus on what's important
The cheerful live longer in years, and afterwards in our affection.
— *Christian Bovée*

Break the barriers
Of course we all have our limits, but how can you possibly find your boundaries unless you explore as far and as wide as you possibly can? I would rather fail in an attempt at something new and uncharted than safely succeed in a repeat of something I have done.
— *A.E. Hotchner*

Seize the summits
The harder you work, the luckier you will get. Never be satisfied with less than your very best effort. If you strive for the top and miss, you'll still beat the pack.
— *Gerald Ford*

Start with a smile

A well-trained dog will make no attempt to share your lunch.
He will just make you feel so guilty that you will not enjoy it.

— *Helen Thomson*

Focus on what's important

I can remember some blurry choices when my children were
young when I may not have attended a play or a soccer game
because I had some conflicting business commitment. It's ironic
that twenty-five years later I can remember I didn't go to that
event, but I can't remember what business thing I was doing. I
wish I had been defined as the father of my children, as someone
who made my community a better place.

— *Randall Tobias*

Break the barriers

The times are bad. Very well, you are there to make them better.

— *Thomas Carlyle*

Seize the summits

The virtue lies in the struggle, not in the prize.

— *Richard Milnes*

Start with a smile
A farmer put an ad in the papers that said, "Need wife who owns her own tractor. Please send picture of tractor."

— *Anonymous*

Focus on what's important
I was guilty of comparing myself with others all the time. I'd look in magazines and look at other models and compare myself with them; same thing with actresses. I had to learn that we are different and just can't be someone else, or even try to be. I had to learn to appreciate myself.

— *Brooke Shields*

Break the barriers
He who asks a question is a fool for five minutes; he who does not ask a question remains a fool forever.

— *Bob Phillips*

Seize the summits
I am not discouraged, because every wrong attempt discarded is another step forward.

— *Thomas Edison*

Start with a smile

I can't get a relationship to last longer than it takes to copy their CDs.

— Margaret Smith

Focus on what's important

The test of a vocation is the love of the drudgery it involves.

— Logan Smith

Break the barriers

We do not understand the intricate pattern of the stars in their courses, but we know that He who created them does, and that just as surely as He guides them, He is charting a safe course for us.

— Billy Graham

Seize the summits

The road to achievement takes time, a long time, but you don't give up. You may have setbacks. You may have to start over. You may have to change your method. You may have to go around, or over, or under. You may have to back up and get another start. But you do not quit. You stay the course.

— John Wooden

Start with a smile

Thomas Wolfe wrote, "You can't go home again." You can, but you'll get treated like an eight-year old.

— *Daryl Hogue*

Focus on what's important

I would not exchange my leisure hours for all the wealth in the world.

— *Comte de Mirabeau*

Break the barriers

You don't have to be in a high-profile occupation to be a person of influence. In fact, if your life in any way connects with other people, you are an influencer. Everything you do at home, at church, in your job or on the ball field has an impact on the lives of other people.

— *John Maxwell*

Seize the summits

People with goals succeed because they know where they're going.

— *Earl Nightingale*

Start with a smile

My wife has just two complaints: first, she's got absolutely nothing to wear. And second, she's run out of closet space to keep it in.

— *Anonymous*

Focus on what's important

We act as though comfort and luxury were the chief requirements of life, when all that we need to make us really happy is something to be enthusiastic about.

— *Charles Kingsley*

Break the barriers

If you don't like the way the world is, you change it. You have an obligation to change it. You just do it one step at a time.

— *Marian Edelman*

Seize the summits

It is not until you have a burning yes inside of you about what is truly important, that you can pleasantly, smilingly, cheerfully, say no to all of that which is urgent, but not truly important. The more we are free from non-necessities, the more we are free to do the more meaningful actions of our lives.

— *Stephen Covey*

Start with a smile

We must believe in luck. How else can we explain the success of those we don't like?

— *Jean Cocteau*

Focus on what's important

It is with trifles, and when he is off guard, that a man best reveals his character.

— *Arthur Schopenhauer*

Break the barriers

Loving means devoting yourself to people, but not to changing them. When I devote myself to the people in my life all our lives improve. While I am telling them how to meet my expectations, no one is happy. As soon as I accept them as they are and start caring about them and trying to make their lives easier, everyone is happier and wonderful things start happening.

— *Dr. Bernie Siegel*

Seize the summits

Duty without enthusiasm becomes laborious; duty with enthusiasm becomes glorious.

— *Artemus Ward*

Start with a smile
Conference: The confusion of one man multiplied by the number present.

— *Anonymous*

Focus on what's important
Marriage is not so much finding the right person as it is being the right person.

— *Charles Shedd*

Break the barriers
One day, in retrospect, the years of struggle will strike you as the most beautiful.

— *Sigmund Freud*

Seize the summits
Planning reduces crisis and lowers your stress; buys you a night of rest without you lying awake, thinking about tomorrow; gives you time to assess whether your schedule for tomorrow is realistic; and allows you to start each day feeling confident and ready.

— *Laura Stack*

Start with a smile
The best way to cure your wife of anything is to tell her it's caused by advancing age.

— Anonymous

Focus on what's important
He who gives to the poor will lack nothing.

— Proverbs 28:27

Break the barriers
Don't undermine your worth by comparing yourself with others. It is because we are different that each of us is special.

— Brian Dyson

Seize the summits
I have learned from speaking to many cancer survivor groups that the watch on your hand no longer says, "tick, tick, tick." It now says "precious, precious, precious." When you understand that, every chapter in your life that you write becomes fascinating.

— Steve Sobel

Start with a smile

I did not say this meat was tough. I just said I didn't see the horse that usually stands outside.

— W.C. Fields

Focus on what's important

Beware a gaudy exterior. The wise will infer a lean interior.

— Charles Simmons

Break the barriers

Socially skilled people tend to have a wide circle of acquaintances, and they have a knack for finding common ground with people of all kinds – a knack for building rapport. That doesn't mean they socialize continually; it means they work according to the assumption that nothing important gets done alone. Such people have a network in place when the time for action comes.

— Daniel Goleman

Seize the summits

You cannot be disciplined in great things and undisciplined in small things.

— General George Patton

Start with a smile
I have heard of a man who had a mind to sell his house, and therefore carried a piece of brick in his pocket, which he showed as a pattern to encourage purchasers.

— *Jonathan Swift*

Focus on what's important
I remember when I dreamed of the day I'd be getting the pay I can't live on now.

— *Tom Wilson*

Break the barriers
He who strikes the first blow admits he's lost the argument.

— *Chinese proverb*

Seize the summits
The man who succeeds above his fellow man is one who early in life clearly discerns his objective, and toward that objective he directs all of his powers.

— *Vince Lombardi*

Start with a smile

The government wrote a startling report on petty office theft, then found out they had no loose-leaf binders left to put it in.

— *Gene Perret*

Focus on what's important

It was her thinking of others that made you think of her.

— *Elizabeth Browning*

Break the barriers

Face your deficiencies and acknowledge them; but do not let them master you. Let them teach you patience, sweetness, insight.

— *Helen Keller*

Seize the summits

Form a mental picture of a time or situation in which you never gave up, a time when you faced your fears and defeated them, or think of someone whose strength inspires you. Store that image in your mind and use it as an inner source of strength when you need to fortify your commitment and determination to achieve your goals and live your dreams.

— *Isiah Thomas*

Start with a smile

A professor is one who talks in someone else's sleep.

— *Wystan Auden*

Focus on what's important

The only ones among you who will be really happy are those who will have sought and found how to serve.

— *Albert Schweitzer*

Break the barriers

Every man I meet is in some way my superior, and I can learn from him.

— *Ralph Waldo Emerson*

Seize the summits

If you want to rev up your motivation to achieve a goal, frame your desired goal in the positive (i.e., weigh 150, rather than not be overweight) and create a clear mental picture of you enjoying your success. For most people, pictures provide more of an emotional charge than words alone.

— *Dr. Suzanne Zoglio*

Start with a smile

The aim of flattery is to soothe and encourage us by assuring us of the truth of an opinion we have already formed about ourselves.

— *Edith Sitwell*

Focus on what's important

The magic formula in human relations is simple – when you begin to dislike someone, do something nice for him.

— *John Sherman*

Break the barriers

There's only one way to maintain your wealth, and that is simply this: spend less than you earn and invest the difference.

— *Anthony Robbins*

Seize the summits

If you can't outsmart people, outwork them.

— *Bill Veeck*

Start with a smile

Have you ever called someone up and you're disappointed when they answer the phone? You wanted the machine. And you're always kind of thrown off. You go, "Oh I uh, I, didn't know you were there. I just wanted to leave a message saying, "Sorry I missed you."

— *Jerry Seinfeld*

Focus on what's important

Staying young is trying out new tastes, new places to go, new styles, keeping an open mind, not settling for what you've always had or always done. Staying young is about keeping a fresh vision of the world, being interested, being stimulated, being motivated, being adventurous.

— *Richard Templar*

Break the barriers

Intuition is given only to him who has undergone long preparation to receive it.

— *Louis Pasteur*

Seize the summits

If your ship doesn't come in, swim out to it.

— *Jonathan Winters*

Start with a smile

Classic: A book which people praise and don't read.

— *Mark Twain*

Focus on what's important

Often the most loving thing we can do when a friend is in pain is to share the pain – to be there even when we have nothing to offer except our presence and even when being there is painful to ourselves.

— *M. Scott Peck*

Break the barriers

We have no right to ask when sorrow comes, "Why did this happen to me?" unless we ask the same question for every joy that comes our way.

— *Philip Bernstein*

Seize the summits

To do anything in this world worth doing, we must not stand back shivering and thinking of the cold and danger, but jump in, and scramble through as well as we can.

— *Sydney Smith*

Start with a smile
Pedestrian: A person who can't find the place where he parked his car.

— Anonymous

Focus on what's important
Don't overplan. See what life has to offer. Too often we hurry past a spectacular sunset in order to be on time for a dreaded, meaningless encounter.

— Richard Enberg

Break the barriers
The mentor is someone who tells you what you may not want to hear in order for you to see what you may not want to see so you can be all you have always wanted to be.

— Don Shula

Seize the summits
Putting off an easy thing makes it hard. Putting off a hard thing makes it impossible.

— George Lorimer

Start with a smile
I spotted my ex-boyfriend at the mall. We had a really bad breakup, and I didn't want to make eye contact with him. Thank God I've had years of waitress training.

— *Kate Mason*

Focus on what's important
The colors in the sky at sunset, the delicate tints of the early spring foliage, the brilliant autumn leaves, the softly colored grasses and lovely flowers – what painter ever equaled their beauties with paint and brush?

— *Laura Ingalls Wilder*

Break the barriers
Hope is the ability to listen to the music of the future. Faith is the courage to dance to it in the present.

— *Peter Kuzmič*

Seize the summits
Thinking will not overcome fear, but action will.

— *W. Clement Stone*

Start with a smile
Cow dung at five feet.
— *Abraham Lincoln, on his choice of weapon when he was*
challenged to a duel

Focus on what's important
Let's be thankful. Thankful for plenty – plenty and more – of things to eat and wear; of shelter and warmth; of beauty. Plenty of things that money can't buy, such as tenderness and inspiration and revelation and insight.
— *Gloria Gaither*

Break the barriers
Your body contains the most powerful drugs in the world to treat any illness. But we can only access these drugs with positive thoughts and good humor.
— *Norman Cousins*

Seize the summits
Don't get caught up with always needing to see instant results from your work. Instead, have faith that there will always be a reaction, because that faith is what allows you to make a life-long commitment toward goodness instead of always looking for the shortcuts.
— *Russell Simmons*

Start with a smile

Lady Astor and Churchill didn't get along. Lady Astor said to Churchill, "If you were my husband, I'd put arsenic in your tea."
He replied, "If you were my wife, I'd drink it."

— *Anonymous*

Focus on what's important

I've learned that winning games, titles and championships isn't all it's cracked up to be, and that getting there, the journey, is a lot more than it's cracked up to be.

— *John Wooden*

Break the barriers

The Pilgrims made seven times more graves than huts. No Americans have been more impoverished than these who, nevertheless, set aside a day of thanksgiving.

— *H.U. Westemayer*

Seize the summits

A vacation gives one a chance to look backward and forward, to reset oneself by an inner compass.

— *May Sarton*

Start with a smile
What should you do when a musician comes to your door? Pay him and take your pizza.

— *Victor Borge*

Focus on what's important
Behave towards your inferiors as you would wish your superiors to behave to you.

— *Seneca*

Break the barriers
Until it's written down, it's not a goal. It may be a wish, a dream, a vision or a hope, but it's not a goal. A goal is a measurable written statement of a definite next step toward the realization of a particular vision. Getting your goals down on paper forces you to clarify and refine them. It helps you to spell out exactly what you want.

— *Laurence Boldt*

Seize the summits
The turning point at which you begin to attain success is usually defined by some form of defeat or failure.

— *Napoleon Hill*

Start with a smile
Funny how a wife can spot a blonde hair at twenty yards, yet
miss the garage doors.

— *Corey Ford*

Focus on what's important
When anger enters the mind, wisdom departs.

— *Thomas à Kempis*

Break the barriers
None of us can see the future, but we can know for sure that
whenever we get there, God will have been there ahead of us.
And as long as He's there, what do we have to fear?

— *Pat Williams*

Seize the summits
In any business endeavor, you've got to keep a laser-like focus
on your goals. When you do, your tactics will be geared to success, not to pleasing people who aren't part of your team. Stop
worrying about the critics and Monday-morning quarterbacks.

— *Joe Torre*

Start with a smile

When they operated, I told them to put in a Koufax fastball.
They did – but it was Mrs. Koufax's.

— *Tommy John, as a Yankee pitcher, recalling his 1974 arm*
surgery

Focus on what's important

The mark of the immature man is that he wants to die nobly for
a cause, while the mark of the mature man is that he wants to
live humbly for one.

— *J.D. Salinger*

Break the barriers

He who sings drives away sorrow.

— *Anonymous*

Seize the summits

I write when I'm inspired, and I see to it that I'm inspired at
nine o'clock every morning.

— *Peter de Vries*

Start with a smile

Predicament: The wage of consistency.

— Ambrose Bierce

Focus on what's important

If you observe a really happy man, you will find him building a boat, writing a symphony, educating his son or growing double dahlias. He will not be searching for happiness as if it were a collar button that had rolled under the radiator, striving for it as the goal itself. He will have become aware that he is happy in the course of living life twenty-four crowded hours of each day.

— Beran Wolfe

Break the barriers

We relish news of our heroes, forgetting that we are extraordinary to somebody too.

— Helen Hayes

Seize the summits

Trust comes from keeping a series of commitments.

— Deanna Berg

Start with a smile
When a man says "fine," he means everything's fine. When a woman says "fine" she means, "I'm really ticked off, and you have to find out why."

— John Rogers

Focus on what's important
Wherever God has put you, that is your vocation. It is not what we do, but how much we put into it.

— Mother Teresa

Break the barriers
Change provides the opportunity for innovation. It gives you the chance to demonstrate your creativity.

— Keshavan Nair

Seize the summits
If you don't invest very much, then defeat doesn't hurt very much and winning isn't very exciting.

— Dick Vermeil

Start with a smile

Anything too stupid to say is sung.

— *Voltaire*

Focus on what's important

When a friend is in trouble, don't annoy him by asking if there is anything you can do. Think up something appropriate and do it.

— *Edgar Howe*

Break the barriers

Vigilantly guard your mind against erroneous and destructive thoughts as you would guard your house against burglars and assassins.

— *Grenville Kleiser*

Seize the summits

Excellence is the gradual result of always striving to do better.

— *Pat Riley*

Start with a smile
The hula dance is simple: you put some grass on one hip, some more grass on the other hip, and then you rotate the crops.

— *Anonymous*

Focus on what's important
Whenever you are confronted with an opponent, conquer him with love.

— *Mahatma Gandhi*

Break the barriers
Moral excellence comes about as a result of habit. We become just by doing just acts, temperate by doing temperate acts, brave by doing brave acts.

— *Aristotle*

Seize the summits
The more decisions you make, the better you're going to become at making them. Muscles get stronger with use.

— *Anthony Robbins*

Start with a smile

The trouble with being punctual is that there's nobody there to appreciate it.

— Harold Rome

Focus on what's important

The family traditions I love the most are the holiday celebrations. I look forward to the planning, shopping and cooking almost as much as the holiday itself. You know, you don't need a lot of money to make it special. Why, when we were children, the best Christmas gifts we got would seem cheap today – an orange in each child's stocking. When I think of Christmas, I can still smell those oranges.

— Sarah Delany

Break the barriers

Never eat while angry, frightened or worried. Your body is simply not in a position to make use of the food when it is on a defensive footing.

— Napoleon Hill

Seize the summits

Successful people know how to say no without feeling guilty.

— Jack Canfield

Start with a smile
I think my neighbor broke up with his girlfriend last night, because he played "Ain't No Sunshine When She's Gone," thirteen times in a row.

— *Wendy Wilkins*

Focus on what's important
We don't laugh because we're happy – we're happy because we laugh.

— *William James*

Break the barriers
Once you are really challenged, you find something in yourself. Man doesn't know what he is capable of until he is asked.

— *Kofi Annan*

Seize the summits
The more detailed your dream, the more power it has.

— *Susan Collins*

Start with a smile

Man is the only creature who spends two-thirds of his lifetime saving up for old age, and the last third denying that it has arrived.

— Anonymous

Focus on what's important

Curiosity is the basic state of a young child's mind. Little people have an intense curiosity about the world around them, an immense hunger to learn and grow, and a wide-eyed wonder about what they observe. I've found that my life is always more joyful when I nurture that wide-eyed spirit in myself.

— Thomas Kinkade

Break the barriers

Eloquence lies as much in the tone of the voice, in the eyes and in the speaker's manner, as in his choice of words.

— François de La Rochefoucauld

Seize the summits

I never met a rich pessimist.

— Allen Breed

Start with a smile
The amount of sleep required by the average person is about five minutes more.

— Max Kauffmann

Focus on what's important
Humility comes before honor.

— Proverbs 15:33

Break the barriers
When someone is pursuing their dream, they'll go far beyond what seems to be their limitation. The potential that exists within us is limitless and largely untapped. When you think of limits, you create them.

— Robert Kriegel and Louis Patler

Seize the summits
There will be times when you will feel alone and deserted, when you will feel weak and doubt yourself and wonder if you are stark raving mad, but if you endure and persevere, eventually you will arrive at your dream.

— Les Brown

Breakthrough Power

Start with a smile
If you can count your money, you don't have a billion dollars.
— *John Paul Getty*

Focus on what's important
People will rarely remember your advice, but they will always remember that you listened.
— *Cara Lawrence*

Break the barriers
Confidence is a plant of slow growth.
— *English proverb*

Seize the summits
The leader is the drum major, the person who keeps a vision in front of people and reminds them of what it is that they're about. People are hungry for leadership. They'll gravitate toward leaders who have a vision. People want to be about good things.
— *Lorraine Monroe*

Start with a smile
My best friend got a truck. But she didn't want to be trendy, so she got a UPS truck. Laugh, but she can park it anywhere. Worldwide.

— Wendy Liebman

Focus on what's important
If you just set out to be liked, you would be prepared to compromise on anything at any time, and you would achieve nothing.

— Margaret Thatcher

Break the barriers
Write down the advice of him who loves you, though you don't like it now.

— Ben Johnson

Seize the summits
None of us will ever accomplish anything excellent or commanding except when he listens to this whisper which is heard by him alone.

— Ralph Waldo Emerson

Start with a smile
I like both kinds of music – country and western.

— *John Belushi*

Focus on what's important
I've had a few arguments with people, but I never carry a grudge. You know why? While you're carrying a grudge, they're out dancing.

— *Buddy Hackett*

Break the barriers
Lean, thin hair, can't be photographed very well, not much personality and so forth. Also dances.

— *Film studio executive commenting on Fred Astaire after a 1928 screen test*

Seize the summits
The man with the capacity for self-discipline can tell himself to do the truly important things first. Therefore, if there is not enough time to go around and something must be neglected, it will be the less essential tasks. It is this man that can carry out his own instructions to do what he says he will do and make himself finish the job which he starts.

— *Ray Kroc*

Start with a smile
A conclusion is the place where you get tired thinking.

— *Martin Fischer*

Focus on what's important
A fascinating and creative interest apart from your work is an absolute essential for happy living.

— *Dr. John Schindler*

Break the barriers
Fire your ambition and courage by studying the priceless advice in the proverbs and wise sayings. They're the shortest road to wisdom you'll ever find.

— *Alexander Graham Bell*

Seize the summits
I long to accomplish a great and noble task; but it is my chief duty and job to accomplish humble tasks as though they were great and noble. The world is moved along, not only by the mighty shoves of its heroes, but also by the tiny pushes of each honest worker.

— *Helen Keller*

Start with a smile
Anyone can do any amount of work, provided it isn't the work he is supposed to be doing at the moment.
— *Robert Benchley*

Focus on what's important
An object in possession seldom retains the same charm that it had in pursuit.
— *Pliny the Younger*

Break the barriers
Some luck lies in not getting what you thought you wanted but getting what you have, which once you have it you may be smart enough to see it is what you would have wanted had you known.
— *Garrison Keillor*

Seize the summits
People don't know all of the behind-the-scenes stuff, and if they did, I don't think anyone would call me an overnight sensation. I'm about two decades in the making and I'm still adding to the design.

— *Derek Jeter*

Start with a smile

Wastebasket: Something to throw things near.

— *Anonymous*

Focus on what's important

If you live within your income, you'll be without many things, the most important of which is worry.

— *William Ayer*

Break the barriers

When you are chopping wood and you have a dull ax you must work all the harder to cut the log. A sharp ax makes easy work. So sharpen your ax all you can.

— *Andy Dolbow*

Seize the summits

Celebrate! Don't wait until you've finished. Don't wait until you've reached your goals. Put a little celebration into every day. Celebrate each step you take toward success. Acknowledging and enjoying the little steps will fuel your enthusiasm to carry on and reinforce your commitment and resolve. It makes the journey as fun and rewarding as reaching the destination.

— *Paul and Sarah Edwards*

Start with a smile

Each year as we stamp and address them,
    And into each envelope stuff,
    At Christmas the very best card trick –
    Is simply just having enough.

                            — *Robert Orben*

Focus on what's important

Contentment is achieved only in the absence of envy.

                            — *Tim Kimmel*

Break the barriers

Life requires thorough preparation. We must rid ourselves of
the idea that there's a short-cut to achievement.

                     — *George Washington Carver*

Seize the summits

You may fail a thousand times, but success may be hiding behind
the next step. You never know how close the prize is unless you
continue.

                            — *Bob Tyler*

Start with a smile
If you cannot get people to listen to you any other way, tell them it's confidential.

— *Patrick Muray*

Focus on what's important
When viewing your spouse's imperfections, don't lose sight of your own.

— *Dennis Swanberg*

Break the barriers
I try to make time for reading each night. In addition to the usual newspapers and magazines, I make it a priority to read at least one newsweekly from cover to cover. If I were to read only what intrigues me – say, the science and business sections – then I would finish the magazine the same person I was when I started. So I read it all.

— *Bill Gates*

Seize the summits
Motivation is when your dreams put on work clothes.

— *Robert Orben*

Start with a smile

Wives are people who feel they don't dance enough.

— *Groucho Marx*

Focus on what's important

If our expenditures on comforts, luxuries, amusements, etc., is up to the standard common among those with the same income as our own, we are probably giving away too little. If our charities do not at all pinch or hamper us, I should say they are too small. There ought to be things we should like to do and cannot because our charitable expenditure excludes them.

— *C.S. Lewis*

Break the barriers

The real key to relieving stress is gaining control over irritants you have the power to change and accepting those you don't.

— *Dr. Paul Rosch*

Seize the summits

Hurry is the weakness of fools.

— *Baltasar Gracian*

Start with a smile
Tomorrow: A husband's greatest labor-saving device.
— *Anonymous*

Focus on what's important
People need loving the most when they deserve it the least.
— *John Harrigan*

Break the barriers
The single most significant decision I can make on a day-to-day basis is my choice of attitude. The attitude I choose keeps me going or cripples my progress. It alone fuels my fire or assaults my hope. When my attitudes are right, there's no barrier too high, no valley too deep, no dream to extreme, no challenge too great for me.
— *Charles Swindoll*

Seize the summits
Today, and every day, deliver more than you are getting paid to do. The victory of success will be half won when you learn the secret of putting out more than is expected in all that you do. Make yourself so valuable in your work that eventually you will become indispensable.
— *Og Mandino*

Start with a smile
You don't care if someone doesn't notice your new haircut.
— Anonymous, why it's great to be a man

Focus on what's important
There is perhaps no greater compliment than to have people light up with joy and anticipation when you walk into a room. This happens mainly to people who bring with them an element of happiness and surprise.
— Leo Buscaglia

Break the barriers
The cure for grief is motion.
— Elbert Hubbard

Seize the summits
The most successful people are the ones who have a passion for what they do. They never get bored, they still look forward to their work, and that's what keeps them going.
— Yogi Berra

Start with a smile
When I was a teenager I used to have a pair of very tight jeans. These jeans were so tight that when I zipped them up my nose got bigger.

— *Rita Rudner*

Focus on what's important
The ideal day never comes. Today is ideal for him who makes it so.

— *Horatio Dresser*

Break the barriers
Aging is a deterioration of connective tissue. The stiffness, shrinkage and drying up of aging occur directly in that great web of fiber that ties us together. What exercise does is resist this stiffening. Age is what makes it tight; movement is what keeps it loose.

— *John Jerome*

Seize the summits
Our doubts are traitors and make us lose the good we might win by fearing to attempt.

— *William Shakespeare*

Start with a smile

I don't know much about being a millionaire, but I'll bet I'd be darling at it.

— *Dorothy Parker*

Focus on what's important

Keep a fair-sized cemetery in your back yard, in which to bury the faults of your friends.

— *Henry Ward Beecher*

Break the barriers

We have no choice of what color we're born or who our parents are or whether we're rich or poor. What we do have is some choice over what we make of our lives once we're here.

— *Mildred Taylor*

Seize the summits

Whenever I make a decision, I start out by recognizing that there's a strong likelihood that I'm going to be wrong. All I can do is the best I can. To worry about it puts obstacles in the way of clear thinking.

— *Fletcher Byrom*

Start with a smile
The trouble with giving advice is that people want to repay you.
— *Franklin Jones*

Focus on what's important
Don't assume you can't be happy unless you're doing what you love most for a living. If that were true, only a tiny portion of the world's population would be eligible for joy. The truth is that deep, abiding joy is available to anyone who learns the secret of pursuing every task with energy and dedication, as though it were a calling.
— *Thomas Kinkade*

Break the barriers
The accomplishments of those born blind are a sure proof of how much the spirit can achieve when difficulties are placed in its way.
— *George Lightenberg*

Seize the summits
The question you must ask yourself is "What can I see that others cannot?" Whatever the answer is, that is what you have the power to perform.
— *T.D. Jakes*

Start with a smile

Resisting temptation is easier when you think you'll probably get another chance later on.

— *Bob Talbert*

Focus on what's important

The worst thing you can do for those you love is the things they should and could do for themselves.

— *Abraham Lincoln*

Break the barriers

Life follows the 95/5 rule. Ninety-five percent of what we worry about will never happen. And 95 percent of the time, if it does happen, the anticipation has been far worse than the reality.

— *Roger Crawford*

Seize the summits

Do you love life? Then do not squander time, for that's the stuff life is made of.

— *Benjamin Franklin*

Start with a smile

Ninety-nine percent of the work of the professional bodyguard consisted of one activity: frowning.

— Martin Amis

Focus on what's important

Anyone can be polite to a king, but it takes a gentleman to be polite to a beggar.

— Jim Shea

Break the barriers

Like any other major experience, illness actually changes us. We think soberly, perhaps for the first time, about our past and future. Illness gives us the rarest thing in the world – a second chance, not only at health but at life itself.

— Louis Bisch

Seize the summits

No tyranny of circumstance can permanently imprison a determined will.

— Orison Marden

Start with a smile

A clever wife doesn't lie about her age: she just says she's as old as her husband, and then lies about his age.

— Anonymous

Focus on what's important

Heaven is full of answers to prayers for which no one ever bothered to ask.

— Billy Graham

Break the barriers

Friendship is a great stimulant. Talk your problems over with others. Laugh with them.

— Napoleon Hill

Seize the summits

I was once asked if there were such a thing as luck in trial law. "Yes," I replied, "but it only comes in the library at three o'clock in the morning."

— Louis Nizer

Start with a smile

If there is another way to skin a cat, I don't want to know about it.
— *Steve Kravitz*

Focus on what's important

I have witnessed the softening of the hardest of hearts by a simple smile.

— *Goldie Hawn*

Break the barriers

Understand that you won't actually ever become the best of which you are capable. That's perfection. We can't obtain perfection as I understand it. But we can work, and work hard, toward obtaining it. If you do that, you will never lose, in sports or in life.
— *John Wooden*

Seize the summits

Once you decide that something is a priority, you give it tremendous emotional intensity, and by continually focusing on it, any resource that supports its attainment will eventually become clear. Therefore, it's not crucial to understand exactly how you'll achieve your goals when you first set them.

— *Anthony Robbins*

Start with a smile

One way to stop a runaway horse is to bet on him.

— *Jeffrey Bernard*

Focus on what's important

When someone hugs you, let them be the first to let go.

— *H. Jackson brown, Jr.*

Break the barriers

The great moments, when the world cheers, are not the moments that count. The ones that count are when it's just you, and people have stopped believing in you. Those are the moments that define you.

— *Bob Greene*

Seize the summits

If the goal is significant, it is inevitable that unforeseen mishaps and emergencies will appear along the way. When the scope and demands of a project are extensive, you can't possibly anticipate all contingencies. These challenges test your allegiance to your goal. By having a deep dedication to your mission, you will keep going when others have given up.

— *Marilyn Tam*

Start with a smile

Husband: A curious mammal who buys his football tickets in June and his wife's Christmas present on December 24.

— Anonymous

Focus on what's important

The rich man is not one who is in possession of much, but one who gives much.

— St. John Chrysostom

Break the barriers

The shoemaker makes a good shoe because he makes nothing else.

— Ralph Waldo Emerson

Seize the summits

If you put off a major task until the last minute, with the excuse that you work better under pressure, you leave yourself no time to do the planning that would produce superior results. You also leave no room for correcting mistakes, locating missing information or incorporating better ideas that might come to you too late to be included.

— Alex MacKenzie

Start with a smile
And on Christmas morning, after the gifts have been opened, what are the kids doing? Playing with boxes and snapping the air pockets of plastic packing material.

— *Erma Bombeck*

Focus on what's important
The joy of brightening other lives, bearing each others' burdens and filling empty hearts is the real magic of Christmas.

— *C. Jones*

Break the barriers
Enthusiasm and persistence can make an average person superior; indifference and lethargy can make a superior person average.

— *William Ward*

Seize the summits
Nothing worthwhile is gained without sacrifice.

— *Gary Player*

Start with a smile
It is impossible to enjoy idling unless there is plenty of work to do.

— Jerome Jerome

Focus on what's important
If you are to retain your joy in life you must find much of that joy in spite of disappointment, for the joy of life consists largely in the joy of savoring the struggle, whether it ends in success or in failure.

— John Silber

Break the barriers
People are like rubber bands: They must be stretched to be effective.

— John Maxwell

Seize the summits
If you look at any list of successful people you'll invariably find they reached the top because they developed good habits, then used them to their advantage.

— Rick Pitino

Start with a smile

Have you ever had one of those nights when you didn't want to go out but your hair looked too good to stay home?

— *Jack Simmons*

Focus on what's important

The life span is short for people who retire, looking for a tensionless state. Life is sustained by tension between where we are now and where we want to be – some goal worth struggling for.

— *Stephen Covey*

Break the barriers

I took violin lessons from age six to fourteen, but had no luck with my teachers, for whom music did not transcend mechanical practicing. I really began to learn only after I had fallen in love with Mozart's sonatas. The attempt to reproduce their singular grace compelled me to improve my technique. I believe, on the whole, that love is a better teacher than sense of duty.

— *Albert Einstein*

Seize the summits

There's no shame in praying for guidance. It's a sign of strength.

— *John Wooden*

Start with a smile
She said that all the sights in Rome were called after London cinemas.

— *Nancy Mitford*

Focus on what's important
In matters of style, swim with the current. In matters of principle, stand like a rock.

— *Thomas Jefferson*

Break the barriers
Life is not about waiting for the storm to pass; it's about learning to dance in the rain.

— *Anonymous*

Seize the summits
You will probably get a larger position than you expect when you begin to do larger things than your firm expects.

— *George Hobbs*

Start with a smile
It's not easy having dyslexia. Last week I went to a toga party as a goat.

— *Arthur Smith*

Focus on what's important
The opportunist thinks of me and today. The statesman thinks of us and tomorrow.

— *Dwight D. Eisenhower*

Break the barriers
Slow growing trees bear better fruit.

— *Jean Moliére*

Seize the summits
Nothing can add more power to your life than concentrating all your energies on a limited set of targets.

— *Nido Quibein*

Start with a smile
You don't own a TV? What's all your furniture pointed at?
— *Joey Tribbiani,* Friends

Focus on what's important
I will speak ill of no man, and speak all the good I know of everybody.

— *Benjamin Franklin*

Break the barriers
People learn the most when teaching others.

— *Peter Drucker*

Seize the summits
Whatever path you follow, do it as though Gershwin had written music to underscore your every move. Romantic and idealistic, yes. But I cannot think of anything in life worthwhile that was achieved without a great desire to achieve it.

— *Neil Simon*

Start with a smile

If I'd known I was gonna live this long, I'd have taken better care of myself.

— *Eubie Blake, on his hundredth birthday*

Focus on what's important

If I had my life to live over, I'd relax. I would take fewer things seriously. I would take more chances. I would climb more mountains and swim more rivers. I'd start barefoot earlier in the spring and stay that way later in the fall. I would go to more dances. I would ride more merry-go-rounds. I would pick more daisies.

— *Nadine Stair*

Break the barriers

One of the greatest discoveries a man makes, one of his great surprises, is to find he can do what he was afraid he couldn't do.

— *Henry Ford*

Seize the summits

Opportunity does not knock; it presents itself when you beat down the door.

— *Kyle Chandler*

About the Author

David Young is a policy advisor to the governor of Texas. He received his Bachelor of Science in Business Administration degree, Summa Cum Laude, from the University of Arkansas and his Master of Business Administration degree from The University of Texas at Austin.

David grew up in Fort Smith, Arkansas. Both of his grandfathers were born before the Civil War. He and his wife, Christina, live in Round Rock, Texas. David has traveled extensively throughout the United States, Canada and Europe, and has visited South America, Asia and the Middle East.

Books Coming Soon

Breakthrough Power for Mothers

Breakthrough Power for Fathers

Breakthrough Power for Christians

Breakthrough Power for Leaders

Breakthrough Power for Athletes

Breakthrough Power for Golfers